C000186639

GATWICK
AIRPORT

GATWICK AIRPORT
THE FIRST 50 YEARS

CHARLES WOODLEY

The
History
Press

First published 2014

The History Press
The Mill, Brimscombe Port
Stroud, Gloucestershire, GL5 2QG
www.thehistorypress.co.uk

© Charles Woodley, 2014

The right of Charles Woodley to be identified as the Author
of this work has been asserted in accordance with the
Copyright, Designs and Patents Act 1988.

All rights reserved. No part of this book may be reprinted
or reproduced or utilised in any form or by any electronic,
mechanical or other means, now known or hereafter invented,
including photocopying and recording, or in any information
storage or retrieval system, without the permission in writing
from the Publishers.

British Library Cataloguing in Publication Data.
A catalogue record for this book is available from the British Library.

ISBN 978 0 7524 8807 3

Typesetting and origination by The History Press
Printed and bound in Great Britain by TJ International Ltd.

CONTENTS

ACKNOWLEDGEMENTS

Thanks are due to the many people who have helped in the preparation of this book:

Harry Hawkins and the Gatwick Aviation Society, for permission to reproduce written material and images from their website and their *Hawkeye* magazine.

Ian Anderson, for permission to reproduce material and images from his article 'Gatwick Hangar History' in the September 2008 issue of *Airfield Review* magazine.

Andrea Hopkins, Media Relations Manager, Gatwick Airport Ltd, for permission to use images from their official website.

Bill Teasdale, for permission to reproduce Peter Fitzmaurice's images.

David Whitworth, for permission to reproduce images from the Tony Clarke collection.

Howard Smith, for supplying aerial photographs and plans.

And the following, for supplying and giving permission to use their images:

Chris England, Mick West, Simon Shearburn, Ken Honey, Brian G. Nichols, Dave Welch, Tom Singfield, Hans de Ridder, John Hamlin. If there is anyone I have omitted, please accept my sincere apologies and thanks.

INTRODUCTION

The story of London's second airport really began in 1930, when two young men who had met whilst learning to fly at Croydon Airport purchased a plot of land near Gatwick Racecourse to develop as a flying field. In August 1930 an aerodrome licence was issued, but only on a very restricted basis and only for an initial period of six months. Despite local objections the Surrey Aero Club held their opening meeting at Gatwick on 4 October of that year with a fly-in and flying display. In 1933 the airfield was purchased by Mr A. Jackaman, whose ambitions also led him to acquire a controlling interest in Gravesend Aerodrome in 1934 and to set up a new company called Airports Ltd to run both airfields. After its take-off and landing areas had been upgraded, Gatwick was re-licenced in the 'public' category in 1934, and its first regular passenger services, to Belfast and Paris, were inaugurated by Hillman Airways. Plans were drawn up for the construction of a new terminal building and apron areas of the latest design, and in July 1935 the airport was closed to aircraft movements to enable work to commence on the redevelopment.

On 6 June 1936 the new airport, which featured an innovative 'Martello'-type terminal building with its own railway station, was officially opened. The opening ceremony was followed by an extensive flying display, and pleasure flights were on offer. Scheduled services to Hamburg, Paris and Scandinavia were introduced by the original British Airways, but waterlogging problems with the grass runways caused this airline to withdraw from Gatwick altogether in 1937. However, the increasing likelihood of another war in Europe within a few years led to an expansion of the armed forces, and in September 1937 Airports Ltd was awarded contracts to run Elementary and Reserve Flying Training Schools at Gatwick and Gravesend. From the following month Tiger Moth and Hawker Hart biplanes were stationed at Gatwick on this work, and from 1938 Airwork Ltd was engaged on sub-contract work for British aircraft manufacturers there as part of the build-up of Britain's forces. On 3 September 1939 Great Britain declared war on Germany. All civilian flying in Britain ceased, and Gatwick's resources were then devoted to the war effort.

During the Second World War Gatwick was used for a variety of activities. The airfield was situated within the Kenley sector of No. 11 Group RAF

Fighter Command, but initially housed RAF light bomber squadrons which had been hastily evacuated from France as the Germans advanced. Later in the war it was used by Lysander and Mustang aircraft in the army co-operation role, and was the launching point for offensive 'Rhubarb' sorties across the Channel into occupied France. It also provided a haven for many damaged heavy bombers on their way back from raids. In 1945 Gatwick was home to various RAF communications squadrons providing transportation for VIPs, and was also used for the repair and servicing of Wellington and Liberator bombers.

The end of hostilities placed Gatwick's future in doubt, but the authorities were persuaded to allow it to remain open as a base for the many charter and air taxi operators that sprang up post-war. In 1946 these were joined by the Ministry of Civil Aviation's fleet of aircraft that were used for testing applicants for commercial pilot licences and for calibrating airfield landing aids. Many war-surplus Dakota transports also arrived, destined for conversion to airline standards by Airwork Ltd. Major air displays staged by the *Daily Express* newspaper in 1948 and 1949 helped to raise public awareness of the airport's existence, and the state airline British European Airways opened its first scheduled services from Gatwick in 1950. In 1952 it was announced that Gatwick had been selected for development as London's second airport and the principal diversion airfield for London Airport at Heathrow. Plans were drawn up for a new terminal building and concrete runway on a site adjacent to the existing airfield, and on 31 March 1956 Gatwick was again closed to all air traffic except the helicopters of BEA so that redevelopment work could proceed.

In June 1958 the new Gatwick Airport was officially opened by Her Majesty Queen Elizabeth II, but airline operators were at first reluctant to transfer their operations to what they perceived as a remote location, despite its brand-new facilities and excellent road and rail links to central London. Things began to look up in 1960 when the closure of nearby Blackbushe Airport forced a number of charter operators to relocate, and several independent airlines amalgamated to form British United Airways, based at Gatwick. One of the airlines moving in from Blackbushe was Dan-Air Services, and Dan-Air and British United Airways were to be responsible for much of Gatwick's growth in subsequent years, including the introduction of scheduled jet services. They were later to be joined at Gatwick by Caledonian Airways, one of the pioneers of North Atlantic charter flights from the airport.

On 1 April 1966 the state-run British Airports Authority came into being and took over the running of Heathrow and Gatwick airports as well as Stansted and some regional airfields, providing some security for the future of Gatwick. New inclusive-tour airlines such as Laker Airways and British European Airways Airtours set up bases there, and British United Airways established a network of scheduled services to Europe, Africa and South America before merging with Caledonian Airways to form what became British Caledonian Airways. In September 1977 Laker Airways inaugurated the revolutionary 'Skytrain' low-fare service to the USA, and other transatlantic scheduled services were soon introduced by British Caledonian and US carriers such as Delta Airlines and Braniff International Airways. In 1978 the BAA-subsidised Gatwick-Heathrow Airlink was set up to address the problem of providing a speedy link between the two airports for connecting passengers. Sikorsky S-61N helicopters made the fifteen-minute trip at frequent intervals until the completion of motorway links to Gatwick made the service redundant. The fifty-year timescale covered by this book brings us to the beginning of the 1980s. By this time the BAA's plans for the expansion of Gatwick included a 'satellite' building to replace the north pier, and a second terminal linked to the original one by a driverless monorail link. These developments and more were to come about in the later part of Gatwick's history, but that is perhaps for another book.

1

PRE-WAR GATWICK

The name 'Gatwick' can be dated back to 1241 and is derived from Anglo-Saxon words meaning 'goat farm'. In that year Richard de Warwick assigned his rights to some land – 4 acres of meadow and 18 acres of other land in the Manor of Charlwood – to John de Gatewyk and his heirs. This land became part of the Manor of Gatwick and was owned by the de Gatewyks until the fourteenth century, when the land was divided up between various families. In 1890 the land that the present day airport lies on was purchased by the Gatwick Race Course Company. A year later Gatwick Racecourse opened, complete with its own railway station named simply Gatwick, which included sidings for horse boxes and was only open on race days.

For three years during the First World War the Aintree Grand National was relocated to Gatwick Racecourse and run over the same distance. A special course of the same length and incorporating twenty-nine fences was laid out, and the event was held at Gatwick in 1915, 1916 and 1917, although it went under another name for its first year there. After 1917 the Grand National returned to Aintree, but racing at Gatwick was to continue until 1940. In the late 1920s a chance meeting between Ronald Waters and John Mockford whilst they were both taking flying lessons at Croydon Airport led to them deciding to go into the aviation business together. Mr Mockford was tied up with his university studies at the time, so Mr Waters went ahead on his own initially and set up a business named Home Counties Aircraft Services Ltd at Penshurst Aerodrome in Kent, which was a designated emergency landing ground for aircraft bound for Croydon, then the country's principal airport. He purchased a small number of light aircraft and gave flying lessons from Penshurst but did not find it particularly attractive. He became aware that an area of farmland of around 90 acres between Gatwick Racecourse and Lowfield Heath was for sale and believed that it would be ideal as a diversion airfield for Croydon in the event of bad weather, so in March 1930 he opened negotiations for the purchase of the land and wrote to the Air Ministry's Civil Aviation Department to sound out their interest.

Before receiving a reply he completed the purchase of the land and on 25 June 1930 submitted an application for an airfield licence and the requisite fee of £1.05. In due course the Air Ministry wrote back stating that they were not interested in taking over the site as an emergency landing ground as it was too far south of Croydon. They did, however, still issue an aerodrome licence effective from 1 August 1930. The licence was restricted to private flying only and was only valid for aircraft in the size category of the Avro 504 trainer biplane.

Furthermore, the licence was only valid for 6 months' duration. The site of the airfield was on low-lying grassland to the east of the threshold of the present Runway 26, extending south through the current southern maintenance area to the site of the future 'Beehive' terminal. The Air Ministry advised that they would not issue a less restrictive licence until more airfield obstructions had been removed, hedges cut down, and an unobstructed take-off and landing run of 500yd was provided in an east-west direction. As soon as the temporary licence was received Mr Waters transferred his activities from Penshurst and that August Bank Holiday weekend he offered pleasure flights from 25p and stunt flying from £1.05. A small hangar was erected for three or four light aircraft, and before the end of August the Surrey Aero Club had been formed, with its clubhouse initially located in a wooden shed attached to the hangar.

There were still some local objections, but these were overcome and on 4 October 1930 the Surrey Aero Club was officially opened with a fly-in attended by twenty-eight visiting aircraft. The programme of events started with a parade and flypast led by Captain Stack in his Moth aircraft. There followed displays of aerobatics, aerial balloon bursting, the 'bombing' of a tractor, and crazy flying. The finale was a parachute descent from a Spartan three-seater aircraft flying at around 2,000ft. The public was officially confined to an enclosure at a charge of 1s 3d (6p), but most of the large crowd of local inhabitants watched for free from the surrounding hedgerows.

In the evening there was a dance at the Timberham Hotel. The airfield was some 90 acres in extent and included a small hangar and two fuel pumps supplying Redline petrol. Flying instruction was available from a Mr Watts of the Home Counties Aircraft Co. On 25 January 1931 tragedy struck. An Avro 504 was aloft from Gatwick and was carrying out aerobatics when it suddenly went into a spin and crashed into a field, killing all three occupants including the ground engineer at Gatwick. The incident made the press, bringing Gatwick some needed publicity, albeit of the wrong kind. At the end of March 1931 the Surrey Aero Club clubhouse was transferred to newly acquired premises at Hunts Green Farm, adjacent to the aerodrome.

Among the improved facilities were sleeping accommodation and tennis courts for non-flying club members. A promotional booklet issued at the time described the new premises as 'probably the finest clubhouse of its kind anywhere'. During 1931 the airfield was increasingly used by jockeys and race-goers flying in for meetings at Gatwick Racecourse and also for (unlicensed and unofficial) weather diversions from Croydon. In May 1932 Mr Walters and Mr Mockford sold the aerodrome to the Redwing Co. Ltd, which, under the name of Redwing Aircraft Ltd, manufactured a two-seater light aircraft at Colchester. The original plan was to move the factory to Gatwick, but in fact the aircraft construction activity remained at Colchester.

However, Redwing Aircraft Ltd did transfer its registered office and sales office to Gatwick and also operated the Redwing Flying School and the Surrey Aero Club from there. Discussions also continued with Imperial Airways and the Air Ministry regarding the possible use as the official bad weather diversion airfield for Croydon, and by the end of 1932 the Air Ministry committed a limited amount of expenditure to this purpose. The official opening under Redwing ownership took place on 1 July 1932 with a brass band performance and guests including the Duchess of Bedford. Another flying display occurred on 19 April 1933, this time organised by Sir Alan Cobham's National Aviation Day Campaign, and during 1932 and 1933 Redwing carried out some airfield improvements with the aim of qualifying for a public licence. But in September 1933 the aerodrome was sold again, this time for a reported £13,500 to Mr Morris Jackaman, who had formed The Horley Syndicate Ltd to acquire the rights and liabilities. In January 1934 Mr Jackaman also acquired a controlling interest in the company which owned Gravesend Aerodrome in Kent. In February 1934 Gatwick's licence was renewed, this time as a 'public' aerodrome, so permitting its use by commercial aircraft. Mr Jackaman renamed his company Airports Ltd and redesignated Gatwick as London South Aerodrome, while Gravesend became London East Aerodrome. At around this time he secured the services of Mr Marcel Desoutter as his business manager, and by the end of February 1934 Mr Desoutter had been appointed a director of the company. In January 1934 British Air Transport Ltd moved into Gatwick from Adlington, near Croydon. Despite its name this company was not an airline but in fact a flying school, and the move was only ever intended to be on a temporary basis, until its new aerodrome at Redhill was ready. The first airline to operate regular services from Gatwick was Hillman Airways, which moved in from Abridge in Essex in 1934 and operated schedules to Belfast and Paris. Hillman later merged with United Airways and Spartan Airways in 1935 to form Allied British Airways (later shortened to British Airways). For some time Mr Jackaman had been interested in the possibility of starting a high-speed hourly air link between Gatwick and Paris, and in January 1935 a Fokker-owned Douglas DC-2 demonstration aircraft was brought over from Amsterdam for trials. After clearing customs at Gravesend it was positioned to Gatwick and was then flown to a point overhead Brighton and back with passengers on board who included representatives from the Southern Railway and the General Post Office. On the outward leg Brighton was reached in eight minutes.

On 16 February 1934, at an Extraordinary General Meeting of Airports Ltd, the company's nominal capital was increased from £200 to £20,000, in units of £1. Later that year the Air Ministry and Airports Ltd arrived at an agreement which provided a firm foundation for the necessary redevelopment of Gatwick. The agreement provided for an annual subsidy to be paid to Airports Ltd over a period of fifteen years, at the end of which time the Air Ministry could purchase the airport. Further development of Gatwick would be under the general supervision of the Air Ministry. Airports Ltd would install night-flying equipment at both Gatwick and Gravesend. The contract stipulated that a terminal building at Gatwick would be completed by the end of October 1935, and that the airport would be ready for night flying by 1 November.

On 8 October 1934 Morris Jackaman submitted a provisional specification to the Patent Office entitled 'Improvement relating to buildings, particularly for Air Ports'. This invention sought 'to provide a building adapted to the particular requirements of traffic at airports with an enhanced efficiency in operation at the airport, and in which constructional economies are afforded'. Various advantages of a circular terminal were detailed, including: 1. Certain risks to the movement of aircraft at airports would be obviated. 2. More aircraft, and of different sizes, could be positioned near the terminal at a given time. 3. A large frontage for the arrival and departure of aircraft would be obtained without the wastage of space on conventional buildings.

The application described the terminal: functioning as the terminus (or station building), administrative offices and base of operations, for passenger or freight traffic, it would be 'arranged as an island site on an aerodrome'. The building itself would be polygonal or circular in form, 'each side or length of frontage being sufficiently long so that space on which it immediately fronts is sufficient for the aircraft to be dealt with'.

The building thus has what may be termed a continuous frontage and the ground appertaining to each side of it may be provided with appliances such as gangways, preferably of the telescopic sort, to extend radially for sheltered access to aircraft. It will be observed that by this arrangement the aircraft can come and go without being substantially impeded by other aircraft which may be parked opposite other sides of the building, and this not only ensures efficiency of operations with minimum delay, but also ensures to some extent at any rate that the aircraft will not for example, in running up their engines, disturb other aircraft in the rear, or annoy the passengers or personnel thereof.

Passengers board British Airways de Havilland D.H.86B G-ADYE for Paris in 1936, using one of the telescopic 'fingers' at the 'Beehive' terminal building. (via author)

In the concluding paragraph it noted that flood-lighting could be arranged 'so that at choice any particular parking space may be lit up with fairly sharp definition, so that passengers will not have any tendency to go to the wrong aircraft, and need not even know of its presence at night'.

In order to finance airport improvements such as night-flying equipment, and to attract more airlines, the original, privately owned Airports Ltd was wound up on 24 May 1935, with a declaration that its debts of some £14,000 would be paid off within twelve months. In its place, a new public company, also called Airports Ltd, was incorporated. The new company had four non-executive directors, and two joint managing directors, Morris Jackaman and Marcel Desoutter. Their appointments were to be of five years duration, at salaries of £1,250 per annum each. On 6 June 1935, 840,000 Ordinary Shares in the new Airports Ltd were made available at a price of 5s (25p) each. The prospectus showed that the company would:

a. Acquire Gatwick (London, South) and Gravesend (London, East) Airports, together with the equipment and buildings erected thereon.
b. Acquire the benefits of the payments to be made by the Air Ministry for the period of fifteen years, in consideration of the installation of night-flying equipment at the company's airports.
c. Acquire the benefit of the agreement made with the Southern Railway Company to build a railway station at Gatwick Airport.
d. Erect a 'Martello'-type terminal air station at Gatwick.

On 1 February 1935 the Air Ministry had renewed the airport licence for a further twelve months, but on 6 July 1935 Gatwick was closed to all air traffic to allow the development work to proceed. This included the installation of airfield drainage and the straightening of the River Mole. A contract was signed between Airports Ltd and the Air Ministry which provided annual subsidy payments to the company over fifteen years. Completion of a new terminal building was specified for the end of October 1935 but problems with mud caused this to overrun.

Despite the airfield being officially closed, the pilots of light aircraft continued to land there quite often, giving Morris Jackaman cause to write to the Air Ministry to complain about this and to pint out that it was causing a hazard to the men engaged on the redevelopment of the site. Negotiations with the Southern Railway over the provision of a new station for the airport had continued, and agreement for this was finally reached in a contract signed on 16 March 1935, with Airports Ltd agreeing to contribute £3,000 towards the cost of a new railway platform on the fast line. The contract also stipulated that Airports Ltd would pay 50 per cent of the cost of making up the roads and footpaths to the station, plus the fences, and 50 per cent of the maintenance costs of these items.

Work commenced at the beginning of April. On 30 September 1935 Tinsley Green (for Gatwick Airport) Station was opened, situated between Horley and Three Bridges and approximately 0.85m south of today's Gatwick Station. Trains running on the electrified line between London and Brighton stopped at the new station almost thirty times daily on the way to Brighton and thirty-six times daily in the reverse direction. The average journey time to or from London was between fifty-one minutes and fifty-five minutes.

The Southern Railway offered cheap day return tickets from London (London Bridge, Victoria or Waterloo) at a cost of 5s 9d (29p) in First Class and 3s 9d (19p) in third class, and there were also special workmen's tickets from Redhill, Earlswood and Horley in third class only (presumably for the use of workers engaged on the construction of the new airport). Tinsley Green Station was renamed Gatwick Airport Station on 1 June 1936.

By the middle of February 1936 the basic framework of the terminal building was complete, and workmen were laying the parquet flooring and beginning the interior decoration. On 15 May 1936, following an inspection, the Air Ministry sent a telegram to Airports Ltd stating that the airport licence would be restored from 17 May, initially until 31 January 1937. A copy of the telegram was sent to the chief constable of the Surrey Police at Guildford, and Airports Ltd approached the Horley and District Cottage Hospital to enquire if 'it would agree to be responsible for accidents in connection with the aerodrome'. Although the hospital had only sixteen beds the request was agreed to at a meeting of its management committee on 21 May.

GATWICK

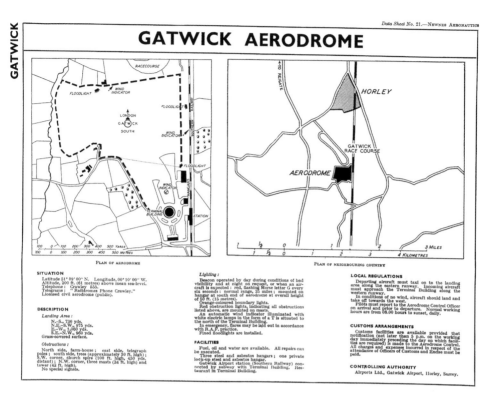

Data Sheet No. 21.—NEWNES AERONAUTICS

GATWICK AERODROME

SITUATION

Latitude 51° 09' 00" N. Longitude, 00° 10' 00" W.
Altitude, 200 ft. (61 metres) above mean sea-level.
Telephone : Crawley 555.
Telegrams : " Raildromes Phone Crawley."
Licensed civil aerodrome (public).

DESCRIPTION

Landing Area :
   N.–S., 720 yds.
   N.E.–S.W., 975 yds.
   E.–W., 1,060 yds.
   S.E.–N.W., 960 yds.
   Grass-covered surface.

Obstructions :
   North side, farm-house ; east side, telegraph
poles ; south side, trees (approximately 30 ft. high) ;
S.W. corner, church spire (100 ft. high, 450 yds.
distant) ; N.W. corner, three masts (24 ft. high) and
tower (42 ft. high).
   No special signals.

Lighting :
   Beacon operated by day during conditions of bad
visibility and at night on request, or when an aircraft is expected : red, flashing Morse letter G every
six seconds : normal range, 25 miles ; mounted on
hangar at south end of aerodrome at overall height
of 50 ft. (15 metres).
   Orange-coloured boundary lights.
   Red obstruction lights, indicating all obstructions
listed above, are mounted on masts.
   An automatic wind indicator illuminated with
white electric lamps in the form of a T is situated to
the north of the Terminal Building.
   In emergency, flares may be laid out in accordance
with R.A.F. practice.
   Fixed floodlights are installed.

FACILITIES

   Fuel, oil and water are available. All repairs can
be executed.
   Three steel and asbestos hangars ; one private
lock-up steel and asbestos hangar.
   Gatwick Airport station (Southern Railway) connected by subway with Terminal Building. Restaurant in Terminal Building.

LOCAL REGULATIONS

   Departing aircraft must taxi on to the landing
area along the eastern runway. Incoming aircraft
must approach the Terminal Building along the
western runway.
   In conditions of no wind, aircraft should land and
take off towards the west.
   Pilots must report to the Aerodrome Control Officer
on arrival and prior to departure. Normal working
hours are from 08.00 hours to sunset, daily.

CUSTOMS ARRANGEMENTS

   Customs facilities are available provided that
notification (not later than 5 p.m. on the working
day immediately preceding the day on which facilities are required) is made to the Aerodrome Control.
All charges and expenses incurred in respect of the
attendance of Officers of Customs and Excise must be
paid.

CONTROLLING AUTHORITY

   Airports Ltd., Gatwick Airport, Horley, Surrey.

1938 plans of Gatwick Aerodrome and its location (including Gatwick Racecourse), with details of the facilities available to aviators. (Author's collection)

Work on the airport complex was completed in 1936. The circular terminal building, which soon became popularly known as the 'Beehive', was a white 'Martello'-style edifice which was designed by architects Hoar, Marlow and Lovett. The descriptive name 'Martello' was derived from the Martello towers, which were small circular defensive forts built in several countries from the time of the Napoleonic Wars onwards.

It incorporated several novel features. Six 20ft-long covered corridors with telescopic canvas canopies attached radiated out from a central concourse, enabling six aircraft to be handled simultaneously. Three of these corridors were used for aircraft arrivals and three for departures. In the space where a seventh corridor could have been was a subway 426ft long which connected the terminal building to the airport railway station and permitted departing passengers to remain under cover from leaving central London until they reached their destination airport.

There were two concrete taxiways, one for arrivals and one for departures. Incoming aircraft taxied along until they reached their specified gangway, disembarked their passengers and then continued onwards in a left–hand circuit

The pre-war 'Beehive' terminal building and taxiways under construction in 1936. In the background is the large British Airways hangar. (Author's collection)

A steam train passes through Gatwick Station, on the London, Brighton and South Coast Railway, circa 1930. (Author's collection)

to either the parking area or the hangars. The circular structure of the terminal graduated from a single storey at the outer limit to four storeys in the centre.

The outer circle was devoted to customs, stores and freight departments and the passenger assembly hall. On the floor above were offices and a restaurant which included an open-air terrace overlooking the landing area. The glass-enclosed control room was at the apex of the building. (The 'Beehive' terminal building is still extant within the south-side industrial area, being a Grade II listed building. In 1999 it was refurbished and used as the headquarters of Gibraltar Airways.)

The cover of a Southern Railway leaflet announcing the opening of Tinsley Green Station on 30 September 1935. (Author's collection)

SOUTHERN RAILWAY

NEW STATION

TINSLEY GREEN

(For Gatwick Airport)

On and from

30th September, 1935

A new Station to be known as Tinsley Green (for Gatwick Airport) and situated between Horley and Three Bridges will be opened for general passenger traffic.

FULL PARTICULARS OF TRAIN SERVICES AND CHEAP FARE FACILITIES.

WATERLOO STATION.

H. A. WALKER,
General Manager.

T.C. 2068 $\frac{7000}{18935}$

Waterlow & Sons Limited, London and Dunstable.

Night-landing equipment at the airport consisted of three weather-protected floodlights, boundary lights and a neon beacon. Two large double hangars were constructed, along with a smaller one which was divided up into twenty lock-ups for private aircraft owners. The first tenant of the hangars was Air Travel Ltd, which specialised in aircraft and engine overhauls. Air Travel's hangar was of 150ft span and was 50ft high. At its sides were two lean-to workshops, each 25ft wide. It was situated close to, and at right angles to the railway line, and adjacent to the 'lock-up' hangar. This company was followed by a new air charter company called Air Touring, operating Miles Falcon Major and Short Scion aircraft.

2

THE FIRST SCHEDULED FLIGHT

Over the weekend of 16/17 May 1936 the original British Airways transferred its base from Heston to Gatwick, taking over one of the double hangars, and began operations from there on 17 May with services to Paris, Malmo (via Amsterdam), Hamburg and Copenhagen. The first scheduled service from Gatwick to Paris departed at 1.30 p.m. on that date, using a de Havilland D.H.86 chartered from Jersey Airways but wearing British Airways livery. Flights to Paris operated three times each weekday at a one-way fare of £4.25 which included first class rail travel from Victoria. The Malmo flights were also operated by D.H.86 biplanes at a one-way fare of £13. The aircraft called at Amsterdam, Hamburg and Copenhagen en route, reaching Malmo just over six and a half hours after leaving Gatwick. Another new route, this time to the Isle of Wight, was inaugurated on 25 May 1936 in partnership with the Southern Railway.

Early in 1936 British Airways had bought out the Continental route interests of Crilly Airways, including four Fokker F.XII aircraft. Later that year they were advertised for sale, and two attempts were made to purchase them for use by the Nationalist forces engaged in the Spanish Civil War. In July 1936 British Airways accepted an offer of £38,000 for the four machines, and at midday on 28 July they departed Gatwick for Spain. En route they landed at Bordeaux and were detained there on the orders of the French Air Minister, who was a supporter of the Republican cause. Agreement was reached between the French and British governments that the aircraft could return to Britain on the understanding that they would not be sold to Spain again. On 2 August they arrived back at Gatwick, having been escorted for part of the journey by French fighter aircraft to ensure that they headed in the right direction. British Airways re-advertised them for sale and quickly received several offers. On 10 August they accepted a bid of £33,000 for the aircraft including spares and four spare engines from a Polish arms dealer, who stated that the aircraft were to be used to set up a new Polish local airline

An aerial view of the original Gatwick Airport in the 1930s, showing the 'Beehive' terminal and apron, the large British Airways double hangar, and the small lock-up hangars. (Author's collection)

to be based in Danzig (now Gdansk). On 13 August, four Polish pilots arrived at Gatwick to collect the aircraft.

After receiving conversion training they departed with the Fokkers on 15 August. The aircraft were later sighted overflying the Channel Islands and it became apparent that their final destination was not Poland but Spain. Two of them made it all the way to Spain, and this time none of them returned to Gatwick.

Gatwick Airport was officially opened on 6 June 1936 by the Secretary of State for Air, Lord Swinton, who arrived from York in an RAF Hawker Hart. After inspecting the buildings, Lord Swinton and his hosts adjourned to the private owners' hangar for the official luncheon and for speeches which were occasionally drowned out by the electric trains of the Southern Railway. This led one speaker to remark that 'this co-operation between rail and air had its drawbacks'.

In his speech, Lord Swinton summed up the new terminal, the world's first circular terminal, by saying, 'We have used Martello towers on the south coast to repel invaders. It has been left to the genius of Mr Jackaman to create a new Martello tower whose object is to attract as many Continental invasions as possible.' The magazine *Flight* prophesied that 'the traffic arrangements alone should be capable of dealing with any increases likely to appear during the next decade and the terminal building is such that any increase in the number of passengers and in the quantity of goods can be dealt with by a mere increase in operating personnel'.

The official guests included the famous aviators Jim Mollison and his wife Amy Johnson, the racing driver Sir Malcolm Campbell, and many foreign air attaches, most of whom arrived in a special train from Victoria Station. Many members of the public also travelled to the ceremony by train, using combined excursion travel and admission tickets which cost 4s 9d (24p) each. Those who came by car caused traffic jams for miles around the airport. A special arrivals competition for visiting pilots saw 100 light aircraft land within a thirty-minute period around midday. The competition was won by Mr R.E.L. Beere in a Puss Moth aircraft, and he was awarded the Gatwick Cup and £15.

The total number of visiting aircraft was in excess of 170, and these were on view in the static park. *Flight* magazine commented, 'Probably never before has there been such a varied collection of aeroplanes, both in type and size, at any flying event in this country.' Joyrides were available in Fokker F.XII, D.H.86 and Rapide aircraft of British Airways, and the only mishap to an aircraft occurred

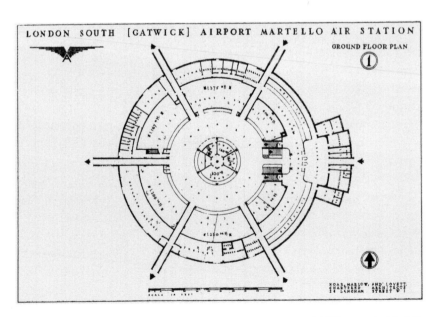

An architect's drawing of the ground-floor layout of the original 1930s terminal building. (Author's collection)

A June 1936 advertisement for Air Travel Ltd's facilities at Gatwick. (Author's collection)

when a de Havilland Moth biplane ran into a depression in the clay surface and stood upon its nose.

After the speeches, Flight Lieutenant Gerald Hill descended by parachute from a Swallow aircraft, bearing a specially composed poem 'Ode to Lord Swinton', whereupon the flags of all the countries served by British Airways were unfurled from the masts in front of the guests' enclosure and the flying display commenced. This included a display by three Gloster Gauntlets of 19 Squadron RAF which 'aerobatted' and landed whilst tied together with ribbons. There was also a parachute demonstration by Mr Clem Sohn, who wore a pair of wings of his own design. During his descent from 5,000ft his main parachute became entangled in the wings. The emergency parachute opened at 200ft but he sustained a fractured arm on landing. After the flying display, pleasure flights were available in British Airways aircraft. For the official luncheon some 700 invitations had been sent out and 487 acceptances had been received. The tables were set for 531 guests but in the event 580 actually turned up.

At the time of its opening Gatwick featured the world's first integrated airport terminal building, combining all the necessary functions in a single structure. During his speech Lord Swinton congratulated Mr Jackaman on the terminal

THE CUISINE OF YOUR FAVOURITE RESTAURANT

Full catering service at all times in the airport building

● **The ideal headquarters for the private owner**

or Airline or Charter Operator. No landing fees for private owners— Restaurant—Snack Bar— Customs Facilities—Social Amenities — Housing — Maintenance — Repairs — and every comfort that the Modern Man can look for.

Second only to the pleasure of flying is the pleasure of eating— with the important proviso that the cuisine and surroundings must be right.

Hence the Gatwick restaurant, where M. Novelli provides a cuisine second to nothing in the West End, from early morning until no one else is hungry —with a free view of the aviation thrown in for those who dine.

Or, for peckish souls, there is a snack bar which contrives to serve something as sustaining as a full meal in the time it takes a waiter to write down your order. So there is no excuse for anyone taking the air with anything but a well-lined stomach and a happy frame of mind.

SPACIOUS LOCK-UPS £25 and £30 p.a.

GATWICK Airport

HORLEY, SURREY

TELEPHONE: CRAWLEY 555

PROPRIETORS: AIRPORTS LTD.

building, but in fact the construction had gone way over budget and this was to lead to a dispute between Airports Ltd and the contractor. This was eventually settled out of court but as a result Mr Jackaman lost his job and Mr Desoutter became the sole managing director.

In July 1936 British Airways began operating night mail services from Gatwick to Cologne and Hanover, from where the Swedish airline AB Aerotransport took over the mails and flew them onwards to Malmo and Stockholm. With the establishment of the night mail services British Airways agreed to man the fire tender and ambulance during the night-time hours. During bad weather and poor visibility a searchlight was mounted on the fire engine, which would be driven along the concrete taxiway followed by the aircraft, as the D.H.86 and D.H.86A aircraft used lacked powerful lighting of their own. By August 1936, Marconi wireless equipment and Air Ministry wireless operators were in operation at Gatwick, but the airport could only be directly contacted by radio at night.

An October 1938 advertisement for Gatwick Airport, emphasising its fine dining opportunities. (Author's collection)

During daytime, inbound aircraft had first to contact Croydon Airport by Morse code to obtain approval to switch to the Gatwick radio frequently.

Despite this complication the introduction of the radio equipment prompted the publication of a pamphlet outlining the advantages of the new airport. This detailed the various landing and parking fees and also included the rules for aircraft using Gatwick, which included:

1. At least half a left-hand circuit must be made before landing.
2. Landings must be made directly into the wind.
3. On landing, aircraft are requested to approach the terminal building by taxiing along the shorter western taxiway, where they will be further directed by the control staff.
4. Pilots should report to the control officer on arrival and prior to departure in order that particulars of load, destination, etc. may be recorded.
5. Departing aircraft are requested to taxi on the landing area by way of the longer eastern taxiway and there to await permission to take off, which is given by a white light directed at the aircraft from the control tower.
6. When a panel bearing red and white vertical bars is displayed on the control tower parapet, aircraft must not leave the hangars without reference to the control officer.

Customs facilities were available from 9 a.m. to 6 p.m. or by arrangement. By September 1936 direction-finding equipment was in use at Gatwick on weekdays, and the 'Lorenz' blind-approach system was on order for installation before the winter.

In the 12 November 1936 edition of *Flight* magazine, British Airways advertised its services as the 'shortest and therefore the cheapest route' to visit the Paris Show being held that month. On weekdays it was possible to leave Victoria Station in London at 9.28 a.m. and travel via Gatwick to Le Bourget Airport in Paris, arriving at 12 p.m. The round-trip fare was £6 15s 0d (£6.75), with a 10 per cent discount to members of 'the aircraft trade and allied industries'.

On 19 November 1936 a British Airways Fokker F.XII was inbound to Gatwick on a night mail service when it struck trees about 4 miles from the airport and crashed, with the loss of the two pilots, although two other occupants survived. The loss of this aircraft, and a previous fatal crash in September 1936, led to British Airways expressing concerns over the distance available for take-offs and the method of communication with aircraft. The service to the Isle of Wight had been losing money since its inauguration, and was withdrawn on 3 October 1936.

In November Morris Jackaman, whose health had been deteriorating throughout the summer, resigned from Airports Ltd. By the beginning of December 1936 passenger traffic on the Scandinavian service had dropped to negligible levels, partly due to passenger dissatisfaction with the cabin heating system on the D.H.86 aircraft used. That winter there was above average rainfall at Gatwick. The newly seeded grass was being used intensively for training flights by the Junkers Ju 52s purchased for the night mail services, and some of the drains collapsed under the volume of take-offs and landings. The pedestrian subway was often flooded to a depth of around 12in, and the British Airways hangar and the boiler house were also affected.

On 17 February 1937 the airfield was declared unserviceable because of waterlogging and British Airways immediately transferred its services to Croydon. On 23 March the airline advised the Air Ministry that it was serving Airports Ltd with six months' notice of withdrawal, as Gatwick had been out of action for six consecutive weeks. Thus ended British Airways' unhappy association with Gatwick as far as scheduled services were concerned. Within a few days of the airline's departure it was decided by Airports Ltd that as an economy measure the neon airport beacon and all the obstruction and boundary lights would be switched off each nightfall, but would be turned on again when required by arriving aircraft. On a more optimistic note, in 1937 a social club for staff and local residents interested in aviation was established at the airport. It was located on the northern side of the terminal building, beneath the restaurant, and the annual subscription was 12s 6d (52.5p) for airport staff and £1 1s 0d (£1.05) for others.

The attitude towards private flyers using the airport had also changed. From 14 October landing fees for private aircraft were abolished, and *Flight* magazine reported in its October 1937 issue:

Although in the days that have passed … the private owner was somewhat naturally discouraged by the owners of Gatwick, whose principal tenant was an airline operating company, British Airways … The private owner found that he was charged landing fees, that the lock-up rents were high and that the law-abiding business of runway taxying wore out his tail-skid and his tyres. He stayed away … During the past month, with official notification of the departure of British Airways and the arrival of Reserve School equipment, the whole policy for the operation of the airport has changed. Messrs Holmes and Kingwill (Air Travel) have joined forces with Airports Ltd and will carry out maintenance work on the Reserve fleet, and the entire atmosphere of Gatwick has already changed quite noticeably. Private owners and club pilots may drop in without fear of rebuff or of tail-skid damage, and new life has already appeared in the form of Mr Paddy Flynn's flying club.

However, the financial position of Airports Ltd continued to deteriorate. A compensation claim for £46,000 from the Jackaman Company was settled out of court, with Airports Ltd agreeing to pay £9,238 plus 14,000 Ordinary Shares.

A March 1938 Airports Ltd advertisement for both its airports, Gatwick and Gravesend. (Author's collection)

At the same time the Southern Railway agreed to release £6,000-worth of securities jointly held with the company.

On 28 July 1936 Penshurst Airfield had closed, and Air Travel Ltd had moved into Gatwick occupying No. 1 hangar with some seventy staff, but in 1937 its assets and administration had been taken over by Airports Ltd. This takeover enabled Airports Ltd to also offer maintenance facilities to civilian operators and to engage in the sale and purchase of aircraft.

Airports Ltd had not been in a strong financial position at the time of the takeover, but its bankers, Westminster Bank, had nevertheless provided the necessary loan, pushing the company's overdraft up to an unhealthy £48,000. However, in mid-September 1937 the company was awarded three-year contracts to run Elementary and Reserve Flying Schools at Gatwick and Gravesend as part of the government's plans to accelerate the training of aircrews for the RAF in view of the possibility of a future war in Europe. On 1 October 1937 No. 19 E & RFTS was opened at No. 1 hangar at Gatwick with six Tiger Moth and six Hawker Hart aircraft and twelve pupils. Additional buildings were also constructed including an operations block, parachute store and machine-gun butts.

RAILWAY AIR SERVICES
SPARTAN AIR LINES

Daily services by Multi-engined Air Liners
BETWEEN

GATWICK AIRPORT
AND

ISLE OF WIGHT

Ryde Airport (with road conveyance to and from Seaview, Bembridge, Sandown and Shanklin), Somerton Airport (with road conveyance to and from Cowes)

SPECIAL FARES FROM AND TO GATWICK
(including Road Transport in Isle of Wight)

SINGLE	ORDINARY RETURN
25/-	**45/-** (available one month)

SPECIAL MID-WEEK PERIOD RETURN
35/-
Available outwards Tuesday, Wednesday or Thursday to return on any Tuesday, Wednesday or Thursday within one Calendar Month.

DAY EXCURSION RETURN TICKET
30/-
Issued for travel from Gatwick on Mondays, Tuesdays, Wednesdays, Thursdays or Fridays, from Isle of Wight on Tuesdays, Wednesdays, Thursdays. Available for return on same day only.

CHILDREN
In arms up to 3 years of age free, if not occupying separate seat.
3 and under 7 years, half full fares.   7 years and over, full fares.

GATWICK AIRPORT Is adjacent to the specially constructed Railway Station served by frequent Southern Electric trains and affording connection from and to Horley, Redhill, Three Bridges, Balcombe, Crawley, Horsham, East Grinstead and Tunbridge Wells.

TERMS AND CONDITIONS OF CARRIAGE
The Conditions under which British Airways Ltd. (the contracting Air Company) undertakes to carry passengers and baggage may be inspected at any aerodrome used by the Company.

FOR TIME TABLE SEE FOLDER obtainable at GATWICK AIRPORT (Phone Crawley 600) and SOUTHERN RLY. STATIONS

Advertisement for the Spartan Air Lines service from Gatwick to the Isle of Wight in the summer of 1936. (Author's collection)

The school undertook the training of RAF Volunteer Reserve pilots, using the Tiger Moths for basic training and the Harts and Hawker Audaxes for advanced work. Most flying training took place at weekends. Later on, the school recruited an additional twelve instructors and added sixteen Miles Magister trainers to the fleet. By October 1938 a new Bellman hangar to house the Magisters was to be completed. In November 1937 the British Airways Transport Pilots' School moved temporarily into Gatwick. Two Fokker F.XII aircraft were used, and the ground equipment, which was housed in the terminal building, included a Link Trainer fitted with Lorenz blind approach equipment.

At the time the British Airways school was regarded as the most advanced in Europe, but on 29 May 1938 it moved on again, to Heston. Shortly afterwards, however, Airports Ltd received an enquiry regarding hangarage from the Airwork General Trading Co., which had been awarded a contract under the new Civil Repair Organisation to give direct assistance to aircraft manufacturers by providing extra manufacturing capacity. One of Airwork's contracts was for modifications to Whitley bombers. They had insufficient space at their Heston base for this, so they leased the former British Airways hangar at Gatwick and spent the summer of 1938 fitting it out for the work on the Whitleys. In September of that year they started work on a second hangar for the CRO work, which was funded by the Air Ministry.

On 17 March 1938 a St Patrick's Day dance was held in the terminal building, and was enjoyed by the 150 guests, who included many of the RAFVR pupils. On 25 June 1938 around 150,000 spectators paid to see the *Daily Express* Air Display at Gatwick. This commenced with low-level passes by an Empire flying-boat, followed by demonstrations of more airliner types including a Lufthansa Focke-Wulf Condor, a SABENA Savoia Marchetti S.M.83, an Air France Bloch MB.220, a British Airways Lockheed Electra and a Dragon Rapide. The RAF contributed displays by Hawker Furies of No. 43 Squadron from Biggin Hill and Hurricanes of No. 3 Squadron from Kenley. The flying also featured a display by a Grumman Gulfhawk aerobatic biplane and such new types as the Fairey Lysander, Fairey Battle and Bristol Blenheim. The climax of the display was a mock raid on the airfield by Fairey Battles of No. 12 Squadron, which was opposed by Hurricanes of No. 3 Squadron and Territorial Army anti-aircraft gun units. In September 1938 Airports Ltd was awarded a contract to train Direct Entry Officers at the flying school it ran for the military, and this brought another sixteen aircraft and eleven instructors to Gatwick. In October 1938 the Insurance Flying Club transferred its activities from Hanworth to Gatwick, where it took accommodation in the 'lock-up' hangar. So did Southern Motors and Aircraft (later renamed Southern Aircraft (Gatwick) Ltd), which moved in from Hamsey Green in the autumn of 1938 and offered repair, modification and maintenance facilities for third parties including Air Touring, and also operated charter flights. These flights ceased in

1952, but Southern Aircraft (Gatwick Ltd) was to continue to offer maintenance services at Gatwick until 1962. By September 1939 Southern Aircraft (Gatwick) Ltd had taken on sub-contract work for Vickers and was producing Wellington bomber components. During the spring and summer of 1939 No. 19 E & RFTS lost examples of Hart, Hind and Magister aircraft in mishaps in the vicinity of Gatwick. On 1 September 1939 all forces reservists were called up for active service. No. 19 E & RFTS aircraft and personnel were transferred to No. 18 E & RFTS at Fairoaks Aerodrome. By this time Airwork were fully engaged in modifications to Whitley bombers, although none had been fully completed. With the declaration of war on 3 September 1939, all civilian flying in the UK ceased and work on civil aircraft at Gatwick was suspended.

3

WARTIME ACTIVITY

In the months following the outbreak of the Second World War, an air of uncertainty hung over Gatwick. Shortly after the commencement of hostilities, Southern Aircraft (Gatwick) Ltd was awarded a contract to carry out Certificate of Airworthiness inspections on all the civilian aircraft at Gatwick, prior to them being impressed into military service. On 6 September 1939 the landing area, the terminal building and the building occupied by the E & RFT School was requisitioned by RAF Kenley, some 5 miles to the north, and Gatwick became situated in the Kenley sector of No. 11 Group, Fighter Command.

One of the first actions to be taken by the newly arrived RAF was the removal of a number of obstruction lights and their supporting pylons, which had only recently been erected at the insistence of the Air Ministry's Civil Aviation Department. These pylons were now considered to be a potential hazard. Despite this, early in December 1939 the British Airways Operations Manager inspected the aerodromes at Shoreham and Gatwick and expressed his satisfaction with Gatwick, in spite of his earlier misgivings.

Early in the New Year of 1940, representatives of BOAC, Air France, HM Customs and Excise, and Immigration Control also visited Gatwick and were of the opinion that it would make an excellent base for civil airline operations. They wanted to take over all the main buildings with the exception of the Airwork hangars, which were busy with important government contracts for the war effort. The problem of operating airline services from a military aerodrome was solved by requesting that the Air Ministry transferred Gatwick to the Air Ministry's Civil Aviation Branch. This was agreed, subject to the proviso that the airlines would have to vacate Gatwick at twenty-four hours' notice if required to do so by RAF Kenley.

Alterations to the terminal buildings were thought to be necessary before any regular services could be commenced, and it was also decided that the obstruction lights, only recently removed by the RAF, should be re-installed

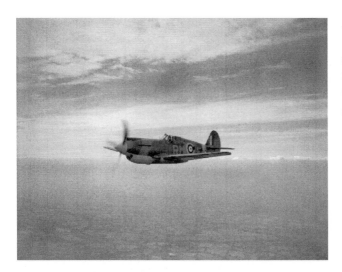

An American Curtis Hawk 81a Tomahawk, serving No. 26 Squadron RAF and based at Gatwick, is seen in flight.

in more suitable locations. Work commenced on the necessary alterations to the terminal, and by May it was well in hand. Over 100 BOAC engineering personnel had arrived, and two Airspeed Ensigns and a Junkers Ju 52 had arrived for overhaul. However, the rapid German advance towards the Channel meant that the proposed airline services could not start, and by the end of August 1940 only thirty-five BOAC staff remained at Gatwick, along with 204 RAF personnel.

During February 1940, No. 92 Squadron, which was in the process of converting from Bristol Blenheims to Spitfires, had arrived from Croydon and set up a training section, only to return to Croydon in May. At the end of May 1940 the HQ Wing of No. 70 Bomber Wing, with its two squadrons No. 18 and No. 57 arrived, having been withdrawn from France due to heavy losses. During their stay they took delivery of replacement Blenheim IV light bombers, but on 11 June No. 57 Squadron moved out to Wyton and on the following day No. 18 Squadron transferred to West Raynham, leaving the Wing HQ to administer the aerodrome.

On 14 June, No. 53 Squadron arrived with their Blenheim IVs and were billeted in the racecourse grandstand. However, on 3 July they too moved on, to Detling. On 15 June 1940 Gatwick Racecourse Station closed, although it was still to be used occasionally after the war, for instance on the dates of the 1948 and 1949 air pageants at Gatwick. The site was eventually to be used as the basis of the new Gatwick Airport Station, which opened in 1958. Also in June 1940, No. 98 Squadron arrived from France, but at the end of July they were transferred to Coastal Command, and later went on to serve in Iceland.

The terminal buildings were once again commandeered during the summer. By September the airfield defences had been greatly strengthened, and a battery of light anti-aircraft guns installed. No squadrons operated from Gatwick during the Battle of Britain, although a number of RAF aircraft taking part landed there to refuel. A number of enemy bombs struck the aerodrome, but without causing damage or injury.

Early in the month No. 26 Squadron arrived with their Lysanders, the first of a long line of army co-operation squadrons to use the airfield. They were later joined by No. 239 Squadron, and both squadrons spent their first three months at Gatwick taking part in army co-operation exercises and providing aircraft for calibration of the anti-aircraft defences.

In October 1940 the role of the RAF station changed when Defiant night-fighters were briefly based at Gatwick. In February 1941 No. 26 Squadron received its first Curtis Tomahawk aircraft to replace Lysanders on army

Corporal J. Fever carries out checks on aerial cameras before they are fitted to planes based at Gatwick.

Instrument fitters install a Type F.24 (14-inch lens) aerial camera in a North American Mustang Mark IA of No. 35 (Reconnaissance) Wing at Gatwick.

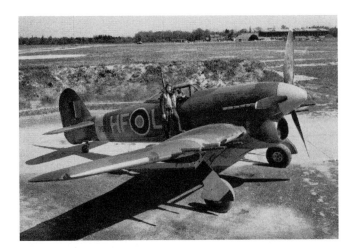

Flight Lieutenant Walter Dring with his Typhoon Mark IB, R8884 'HF-L', at Gatwick.

co-operation duties, and it was joined by No. 239 Squadron in June 1941. Problems with the serviceability of the Tomahawks resulted in No. 239 Squadron receiving six Hawker Hurricane IICs in January 1942.

In September 1941 work on installing a number of gun emplacements and laying wire-mesh army track runways 4,200ft and 3,600ft long was completed, and Gatwick Racecourse was finally belatedly requisitioned. There was also a 3,600ft grass runway. During the following month No. 803 Road Construction Company arrived from Iceland to improve the runways. Since the outbreak of war the resident civilian contractors had continued their activities relatively undisturbed. When BOAC withdrew from Gatwick, Airwork took over the No. 1 hangar for Whitley repairs and modifications, and Southern Aircraft were granted contracts for rebuilding Hawker Harts and Fairey Battles.

In January 1942 No. 26 Squadron was allocated the first P-51 Mustang aircraft to be made available for army co-operation assessment, and trials were carried out at Gatwick. Early in May 1942 this squadron operated the first 'Rhubarb' interdiction sorties using Mustangs, and from July No. 239 Squadron also began using Mustangs on operations. On 19 August 1942 four squadrons of Gatwick-based Mustangs played an active part in Operation *Jubilee*, the raid on Dieppe, providing tactical reconnaissance in support of the landings. On 2 October 1942 Gatwick saw the arrival of the first USAAF B-17 bomber to force-land on the airfield. The aircraft, named *Phylis* and based at Chelveston in Northamptonshire, had three wounded crew members and a reporter from *Time* magazine on board. At that time, the Hollywood film director William Wyler was in England to make a documentary movie about the US 8th Air Force. He was interested in using the story of the crew of *Phylis* and her mission as the basis for his film, but various

Airmen of the Photographic Section of No. 26 Squadron RAF record details on the film magazine removed from a Type F.24 aerial camera, following a tactical reconnaissance training sortie.

A Curtiss Tomahawk Mark IIA, AH896 'RM-Y', of No 26 Squadron RAF, based at Gatwick, in flight.

difficulties arose, and in the end he transferred his attentions to Bassingbourn Airfield and another B-17 named *Memphis Belle*.

Throughout the latter part of 1942 a number of squadrons sent detachments to Gatwick to gain operational experience, but by the second half of 1943 the airfield was left without a resident squadron and was reduced to 'care and maintenance' status. It was, however, still visited by many aircraft diverting in

Tomahawks of No. 26 Squadron RAF, based at Gatwick, in flight.

after raids, including Halifaxes, Stirlings, Lancasters, B–17s and P–47s. Gatwick was selected as the site for one of the new series of 'Darkie' homing beacons for aircraft returning from the Continent, this feature becoming operational in early October 1943.

This marked the beginning of a new flurry of activity, with Spitfire and Mustang squadrons being detached for varying periods. In March 1944 Gatwick was transferred to the Biggin Hill Sector as part of the 2nd Tactical Air Force. In the weeks leading up to D-Day three squadrons were engaged on photographic and reconnaissance missions using Spitfires, Mustangs and Mosquitos.

With the commencement of the V1 rocket bombardment in July 1944 a balloon barrage to protect London was erected, this coming to within 2,000yd of Gatwick. No squadron operations were carried out during this period, but the airfield was still designated as an emergency landing ground. One aircraft to make use of this facility was a Dakota that had lost 6ft of one wing when it flew into a balloon cable over nearby Redhill. A number of casualties from the fighting in France were airlifted into Gatwick during this period.

In January 1945, No. 1337 Wing of Supreme Headquarters Allied Expeditionary Force (SHAEF) was formed at Gatwick, and on 1 February the airfield taken over by the SHAEF Disarmament Unit. Later that month the UK Detachment of No. 85 Group Communications Squadron moved into Gatwick from Northolt and operated regular services to Continental Europe, and during March many high-ranking officials passed through.

After the ending of hostilities in Europe, Gatwick became a satellite of Dunsfold. In June 1945, No. 103 Air Disarmaments Wing took over control of the airfield from the SHAEF unit. This marked the start of one of the busiest periods in Gatwick's history so far, with frequent visits from the Ansons of the communications squadrons and also visits by other aircraft including a Gloster Meteor jet fighter. Number 49 Maintenance Unit was engaged in servicing Mosquitos, and there was even a museum of captured German weapons and equipment at Gatwick.

By October 1945 the volume of traffic had fallen but the airfield still saw a steady stream of VIP flights, with Gatwick being designated as the sole UK terminal for these flights. In 1946 a rundown of RAF activities took place and in July all local Air Ministry contracts were cancelled. On 31 August 1946 RAF Gatwick was de-requisitioned. Meanwhile, the Civilian Repair Organisation work at Gatwick had continued into the latter stages of the war, with Airwork repairing Wellingtons during 1941–43 and also undertaking the scheduled servicing of Liberators from 1943 to 1945. Southern Aircraft, whose wartime staff had grown to over 2,000, were engaged in the repair of Beaufighters and also assembled Stinson Reliants and Beech Expeditors for the Royal Navy.

4

WARTIME PROPOSALS FOR POST-WAR DEVELOPMENT

During 1943 Marcel Desoutter commissioned a report from the well-known airport architects Norman and Dawbarn, which envisaged four possible schemes for the post-war commercial development of Gatwick Airport. These were outlined in the 25 November 1943 issue of *Flight* magazine:

1. The 'small' or 'local' scheme, involving no disturbance to the London–Brighton road, the existing airport buildings or the River Mole.
2. The 'continental' scheme, involving diversion of the London–Brighton road, the removal of Gatwick Racecourse and its associated buildings, and the culverting or diversion of the River Mole for some 1,400 yards. Two parallel main runways to be built, each of 2,500 yards in length, and two subsidiary runways at right angles to these, of 1,450 yards and 1,500 yards in length. The removal of the racecourse would allow the existing Racecourse Halt station to be upgraded for use as the main railway station for the airport. Total area of scheme 1,180 acres.
3. The 'trans-Atlantic' scheme, involving the diversion of the London–Brighton road between its northern limit at Povey Cross and its southern limit at Crawley, and taking in everything between this convex western boundary and the existing Southern Railway, which would form its eastern boundary. Included a proposed new terminal building some 400ft from the railway line with a continuous canopy some 1,500ft long. The terminal and the railway station to be connected by a raised walkway. It was agreed that the development of transatlantic air services should be regarded as a special case, with its own particular airport requirements, and may not best be served from a site south of London. Nevertheless, it was felt that the 'communications and potentialities' of Gatwick were such as to make it worthwhile noting the

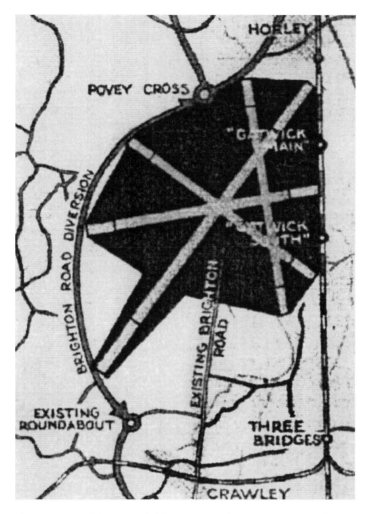

A November 1943 diagram of the proposed 'Transatlantic' layout for the airport, showing how the London–Brighton main road would be diverted. (Author's collection)

physical possibilities of establishing a transatlantic airport there. A plan map published with the report indicated one main surfaced runway of 4,000yd in the direction of the prevailing wind, and three other surfaced runways each of 3,000yd. The total lengths between the boundaries would be 6,000yd and 4,000yd respectively, and it would be possible to surface these full lengths if the overruns so obtained were necessary to ensure 100 per cent regularity of operation for all land-based aircraft types that could be envisaged for future transatlantic use.

4. The 'two-stage expansion' scheme. A partial development of the 'continental' scheme. General layout to be the same, differing only in the length of the runways. Scheme to absorb the greater part of the racecourse to the north. Some deviation of the road from Lowfield Heath on the southern boundary necessary, but western boundary would be the existing London–Brighton road and northern boundary would be the existing course of River Mole. Initial runway lengths would be the same as for the 'local' scheme, but the design would allow for future expansion.

The report also suggested that airports serving London should be located so that each one could serve its own destinations without the need for overflights of London. Included was a diagram showing the proposed natural division of air traffic between Fairlop (Essex), Heston and Gatwick airports. It was acknowledged that some of the world's air traffic would continue to be carried by flying-boat, but the opinion was expressed that the 'extreme difficulty' of finding ideal sites for marine airports in the southern half of England would result in an increasingly greater proportion of post-war air traffic being carried in land-based aircraft as adequate world facilities are provided.

5

THE IMMEDIATE POST-WAR YEARS

Throughout its early post-war history Gatwick was continually under threat of closure. At the beginning of 1945 an Air Ministry official had advised Marcel Desoutter that he was at liberty to dispose of the land the airport stood on, only to later ask him unofficially to hold on to the land for the time being. In April 1945, at a meeting chaired by the Minister of Civil Aviation, Lord Swinton, officials reached a decision that Heathrow in Middlesex and Fairlop in Essex should be developed as the long-term airports for London. Gatwick was specifically rejected, even for the short-term, so it is not surprising that after its de-requisitioning in August 1946 it was largely ignored by those responsible for meeting London's civil airport requirements.

It was returned to the Ministry of Civil Aviation (MCA), but its lack of hard runways did little to attract civilian operators. However, after some urging from Mr Desoutter, the MCA approved his idea of contacting all the UK air charter companies to promote Gatwick as a base for charter and air taxi operations. The response from these companies was very encouraging, with sufficient applications being received to utilise all the accommodation currently available at the airport.

As a result the government decided to requisition Gatwick again, and to licence it for an experimental period of six months for charter operations. The MCA provided the necessary services, and Gatwick once again became a customs airport in November 1946. At that time the airport's grass surface was considered to be capable of supporting aircraft of up to 25,000lb all-up weight. *Flight* magazine reported that some ten companies had arrived or were shortly to move in, but until the necessary redecoration of the terminal was completed (some time in early 1947) the situation was likely to be difficult from the accommodation point of view.

In 1947 Aerocontacts Ltd was established at Gatwick by Squadron Leader H.K. Hughes DFC, a former fighter pilot, and specialised in the purchase, overhaul and sale of aircraft and components. In the early 1950s Aerocontacts Ltd was to become the British Commonwealth concessionaire for the SNCASO Bretagne airliner, bringing an example over to Gatwick in October 1952 for ground inspection and flight demonstration to potential buyers.

A 1949 advertisement for travelling to the airport via Gatwick's own railway station. (Author's collection)

A July 1948 advertisement for Gatwick's rail links with London and the south coast. (Author's collection)

Aerocontacts also became the UK agents for the Piaggio P.136 amphibious aircraft, the Piaggio P.148 trainer, and a jet booster unit containing a Turbomeca Palas turbojet engine which could be fitted to Bretagne, Curtis Commando, and Dakota transport aircraft. The company later acquired the UK distribution rights for the SAAB Safir light aircraft. In 1961 Aerocontacts Ltd moved its UK premises to Gatwick House, some 2 miles away from the airport, as its main business by then was the supply of aviation ground equipment.

In addition to the based engineering companies Airwork Ltd and Southern Aircraft Ltd, the first airline operators to operate from Gatwick after the Second World War included C.L. Air Survey, Dennis Aviation and Bond Air Services. Bond Air Services commenced charter operations in 1946 using single-engined Auster and Percival Proctor aircraft. In 1947 they upgraded to four-engined Handley Page Halifax transports which were used to transport fresh fruit and other produce to the UK from the Continent. Among other operations that year, these machines made seven flights from Caen in Normandy to Gatwick transporting Camembert cheese and five flights from Valencia to Gatwick carrying mandarin oranges.

The company also used a four-engined D.H.86B biplane on many passenger charters out of Gatwick from July onwards. After taking part in the Berlin Airlift, Bond transferred their operating base to Southend. Hornton Airways was formed at Gatwick in 1946 with Proctor equipment and went on to operate Airspeed Consuls and Rapide and Dakota aircraft before ceasing operations in 1950.

An unusual operator from Gatwick in the early post-war years was the Windmill Theatre Transport Co. Ltd, which commenced operating a Percival Proctor aircraft on behalf of the famous Windmill Theatre in London in November 1946. Two years later a de Havilland Rapide was acquired. This was

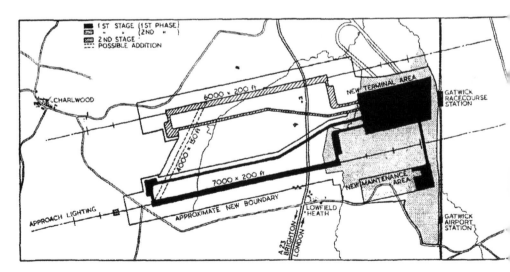

A 1953 diagram of the proposed new terminal facilities and runway layout at Gatwick. The area of the existing aerodrome at that time is shown shaded. (Author's collection)

A 1953 advertisement for the Silver City Airways car-ferry service between Gatwick and Le Touquet. (Author's collection)

flown from Gatwick on trips connected with theatre business, and also on commercial charter flights, by Mrs Zita Irwin, a former Air Transport Auxiliary pilot. The Proctor was disposed of in 1955, but the Rapide was to continue in use on charter flights until 1960, when it was sold and the company was wound up.

Another small operator was Transcontinental Air Services, which was established at Gatwick in 1947 with an Airspeed Consul aircraft, but went out of business in 1949. In March 1947 Hunting Air Transport moved in from Luton and became the first Gatwick-based operator to acquire post-war British-designed aircraft when it took delivery of a de Havilland Dove and two Vickers Vikings. On 8 May 1947 the Dove operated a charter flight from Gatwick to Jersey for the Jersey Motor Races, but the company transferred its operations to Bovingdon Airfield in Hertfordshire with the delivery of the Vikings.

During 1946 the Ministry of Civil Aviation Fleet (soon to be renamed the Ministry of Civil Aviation Flying Unit) moved into Gatwick with its fleet of seven aircraft including Avro 19s, Airspeed Consuls, Proctors and Austers, and a Tiger Moth biplane. The fleet was gradually expanded and was used for the checking of aerodrome facilities and the practical testing of applicants for the pilot's B Certificate. During 1946 the unit calibrated sixteen ground stations and tested 243 pilots. This latter figure rose to 880 for the year 1947. All the unit's aircraft were maintained by Airwork.

In July 1947 twelve aircraft were in use, comprising six Avro Ansons, and two examples each of the Proctor, Auster and Tiger Moth. Squadron Leader A.D.C. Carroll had eight ex-RAF Qualified Flying Instructors under his command, with four more in the process of recruitment. By 1949 the unit was operating twenty-seven aircraft, but then transferred its operating base to Stansted in Essex.

By January 1948 Airwork had received contracts from many operators for the conversion of war-surplus Dakotas to airline standards. All BEA's Dakotas were passing through Gatwick for civil conversion work and Certificate of Airworthiness checks, and conversions were also in hand for aircraft of KLM, BOAC and Aer Lingus. At one point in January 1948 there were thirty-five Dakotas with Airwork, and the company had carried out 253 scheduled overhauls during the previous six months. On 29 April 1948 Dakota G-AIJD of Ciro's Aviation, which had been converted and civilianised by Airwork at Gatwick, won the first prize in the Concours d'Elegance competition at the Cannes International Air Rally.

Airwork's final contract at Gatwick was for the scheduled servicing and repair of F-86 Sabre fighters of the RAF. Large numbers of these arrived on 'Queen Mary' road trailers from bases in West Germany. On completion of the work they were transported by road to Dunsfold, where they were assembled and test flown. At the peak of this activity Airwork employed more than 550 staff at Gatwick, but they were to cease operations at the airport in February 1959.

In spite of increased operations and substantial government investment the future of the airport still remained far from secure, and decision to proceed with the creation of a new town at Crawley added further complications. Crawley Development Corporation was alarmed at the prospect of the expansion of its airport neighbour. After several meetings, assurances were given that Gatwick would not be developed as a major international airport and would be restricted to charter and air taxi work, private flying, and weather diversions from other airports.

Despite this limitation on its activities, in 1948 Mr Desoutter published a twenty-page booklet proclaiming the advantages of Gatwick Airport and listing the facilities offered to potential new operators. In February 1948 the Ministry advised Airports Ltd that it intended to de-requisition the airport (again) in September 1949 and that it proposed removing the telecommunications and other services it currently provided. This resulted in Airports Ltd warning shareholders in its annual report for 1948 that 'it may be necessary to seek alternative uses for the land if support for the airport was not forthcoming'.

However, on 18 March 1948 BEA wrote to the Controller of Ground Services at the Ministry of Civil Aviation, requesting that Gatwick be designated as the primary diversion airport for London instead of Stansted. BEA's interest in the use of Gatwick brought about another deferment of the de-requisitioning process, initially until 1 February 1950, and then for an indefinite period.

On 19 June 1948 the Royal Aero Club staged an air rally at Gatwick which was attended by twenty-six aircraft from seven countries despite poor weather conditions. Among the aircraft was an Airspeed Consul belonging to the Duke of Almodovar, a Lockheed 12A from Belgium, an Auster V from Spain, and three Piper Supercruisers. A similar event but on a larger scale took place in early July that year when the *Daily Express* newspaper staged its Air Pageant at Gatwick.

Despite dull and cold conditions and a cloudbase of around 1,500ft, the pageant attracted around 60,000 spectators to see a varied display, which commenced with demonstrations of various light aircraft and formation flypasts by six Meteors and six Vampires, followed by an aerial procession of civil airliners. These included: a KLM Douglas DC-6, a BEA Vickers Viking, a BSAA Avro Tudor IV, an Air France Languedoc, a Skyways Avro York, a BOAC Short Solent flying-boat, and an Olley Air Service Dove.

The flypasts were concluded by six Avro Lincoln bombers in two 'vics' of three. Aerobatics were provided by a formation of four Vampires and a solo Meteor. The Royal Navy provided displays by Sea Furies and Sea Hornets, and helicopters were represented by examples of the Sikorsky S-51 and the Hoverfly 2. There was even a live demonstration of the Martin-Baker ejector-seat, with Mr Bernard Lynch being fired from a Meteor in cloud.

On the commercial front, on 17 August 1948 over 10 tons of Camembert cheese was flown into Gatwick aboard three French Dakotas. The UK airline Air Transport Charter (CI) was operating Gatwick–Jersey services at this time, but was restricted to using Rapide biplanes as its Dakotas were engaged on the Berlin Airlift and on carrying milk in churns from Ireland into Liverpool to cope with a shortage. The success of the 1948 Air Pageant inspired the *Daily Express* to repeat the event in July 1949, this time in near-perfect weather and attended by up to 90,000 spectators, who each paid 2*s* 6*d* for admission.

The highlights of that year's event included fly-pasts by three Sunderland flying-boats, nine B-29 Superfortresses of the 509th Bomb Group USAF, six Avro Lincolns, and five Hastings transports of No. 38 Group, RAF. The aerobatic displays included those by four Stampe SV.4C biplanes of the French 'Patrouille d'Etampes' team, and a solo Pitts Special biplane flown by Miss Betty Skelton from the USA.

The next decade started well for Gatwick, with over 11,000 passengers and 169 tons of freight passing through in 1950, many no doubt on a new Gatwick–Alderney summer service using Rapide biplanes, which started in April. This was BEA's first scheduled service from Gatwick, and was to last until the end of the 1952 summer season. For these flights BEA did not station any staff full-time at Gatwick. Instead, a traffic clerk was sent down from the airline's Kensington Air Station in West London to oversee each movement.

However, the next two years saw a drastic decline in traffic at Gatwick, earning the airport the reputation of being a 'ghost airfield'. A review of the operations in January 1950 would show the airport in use by only seven charter companies, as well as being the principal diversionary airfield for Croydon, some 14 miles to the north. Gatwick closed at dusk each day and was restricted to aircraft types not exceeding 10,500lb all-up weight. It was still owned by Airports Ltd, but was controlled by the Ministry of Civil Aviation.

Three runways were operational, one running south-west to north-east and covered in steel mesh, another steel mesh strip aligned east–west, and a grass runway running south-east to north-west. The first mentioned runway was 1,400yd long by 50yd wide, and the others were 1,200yd long and 50yd wide. A concrete perimeter track with hardstandings surrounded the whole airfield, with taxiways leading to the terminal buildings and hangars.

In mid-July 1951 the airport played host to the International Invitation Air Rally, organised by the Royal Aero Club. Thirty-five assorted light aircraft arrived from seven countries in Europe and beyond, with the longest journey being made by a Fairchild Argus from Oran in Algeria. Other types attending

Percival Proctor *G-AHEU* at Gatwick in 1955. (Peter Fitzmaurice via Bill Teasdale)

included Austers, Cessnas, Ercoupes, and a two-seater Junkers Junior from Finland. After partaking of refreshments on the terrace of the terminal building, the human participants went on to a ball at Londonderry House in London before setting off the following day on the next leg of the rally, to Sherburn-in-Elmet in Yorkshire.

A significant event during September 1951 was the transfer to Gatwick from Peterborough of the BEA Helicopter Experimental Unit. The unit was equipped with three Sikorsky S-51s and two Bell 47B3s, and during its early days at Gatwick it continued its work of evaluating helicopter navigational, blind-flying and approach aids. A trial scheduled service between Heathrow and Birmingham was also operated by the Gatwick-based machines. In subsequent years the unit took delivery of Bristol 171 and Sikorsky S-55 equipment and Gatwick became the central servicing base for all BEA helicopters.

On 22 December 1954 newly acquired Westland-Sikorsky WS-55 helicopters entered BEA service on a new Gatwick–London Airport–Southampton route.

On the first day of operation just three passengers were carried from Gatwick to London Airport, and just one on the Southampton–Gatwick leg.

In 1952 Silver City Airways commenced car-ferry operations from Gatwick, using Bristol 170s on a route to Le Touquet in France. By April 1955 larger Bristol 170 Mk 32 Superfreighters were in use. Services were flown twice-daily during the summer season, and each aircraft could carry three small cars and twenty passengers or three larger cars and twelve passengers. For foot passengers there was a rail connection at Le Touquet into Paris. The car-ferry services from Gatwick were finally axed in 1967.

Also in 1952, Jersey Airlines had their application for services between Gatwick and Jersey approved. Their service was operated initially by Rapide biplanes, but from 1953 new Heron aircraft were used. In a memorandum to the Cabinet dated 22 July 1952, the Ministry of Civil Aviation announced that:

> Gatwick, however, needs complete reconstruction if it is to accept large aircraft diverted from London Airport, which it must be able to do. This will mean spending about £2 million by the end of 1955 and about £4 million during the following five years. Of this expenditure about two thirds of a million pounds will pay for itself through hangar rents. Against the rest can be set the savings to the Government from giving up the other airports (Northolt, Croydon, Bovingdon and Stansted) – about £750,000 in capital and £400,000 per annum in operating costs. There will also be earnings from landing fees, office rents, concessions etc.

In early October 1952 the MCA announced that Gatwick had been chosen from over fifty locations including Blackbushe, Dunsfold, Stansted and Biggin Hill for development to meet the future needs of London's air traffic. It was estimated that air movements in the London area would double by 1960 and that London Airport alone would not be able to cope with such an increase.

There was also a requirement for an alternative diversion airport which had ready access to London and was capable of handling all the types of aircraft flying into London at that time, as well as accepting the transfer of some southbound scheduled services. Meteorological records showed that on days when visibility at London Airport was below the normal 'diversion level' (visibility of less than 550yd and/or 5/8 clouds or more at 300ft), visibility at Gatwick was on average above that level on 55 per cent of the occasions covered.

With regards to the other alternative airports, it was considered that Blackbushe was too close to the airfield at Farnborough and that in the prevailing westerly winds its traffic pattern would conflict with that of London Airport at Heathrow. Dunsfold's access to London was markedly inferior, and although it could be developed at slightly less cost than Gatwick it was still required for test flying by the Hawker Aircraft Co. and for military activities. Like fellow candidate Bovingdon in Hertfordshire, the airfield at Stansted was on the wrong side of London and was one and a half to two hours by road or rail from the capital. Biggin Hill and West Malling in Kent were needed by the RAF, and Croydon and Fairlop in Essex were in heavily built-up areas.

The proposed development of Gatwick would be carried out in two stages. A new northern runway, aligned on heading 09/27 and 7,000ft long by 150ft wide, was to be completed by 1956. The runway would incorporate high-speed turn-offs on to taxiways, the first such in Britain, and its eastern end would be sited 3,700ft from the railway line.

By this time the necessary diversion of the A23 London–Brighton road would have been carried out. This would isolate the 'Beehive' terminal area, but the work of the BEA Helicopter Experimental Unit would be unaffected. Gatwick Airport Station would be closed, and the currently out-of-service Gatwick Racecourse Station would be re-opened as Gatwick Airport Station, and redeveloped to serve the new airport complex.

The second stage of the development would not start before 1958 and would include the construction of a second parallel runway to the south of the new terminal area. This runway would be 7,000ft long by 200ft wide. A new terminal building would be built between the eastern ends of the two runways and adjacent to the new Gatwick Airport Station. The original terminal area in the south-east corner of the site would be redeveloped as a new maintenance area.

At the time of the announcement of the proposals the MCA estimated that as few as fifty houses would need to be demolished to make way for the redevelopment. A year later a modified plan was produced as the result of consultations with the local authorities, the Crawley Development Corporation and the Railway Executive. Under this new plan both runways would be relocated westwards by about half a mile. The southern runway would be built first, with the northern runway following later if justified by the volume of traffic. These changes would render the expensive westerly diversion of the London–Brighton road unnecessary. Instead, it was proposed to divert the road along the eastern boundary of the airport immediately to the west of the runway, thus combining access to the airport terminal building with local access to the railway station.

It was not the intention to use Gatwick Airport all year round. Its principal purpose was to receive diversions from London Airport, and to operate some short-distance seasonal scheduled services and charter flights. In November 1953 the Airwork canteen at Gatwick was the venue for a meeting to explain the government's case for selecting Gatwick as the alternative airport for London.

Around 500 local residents attended, and they were generally opposed to the development.

On 2 December 1955 the first two contracts for the development of Gatwick were announced by what had now become the Ministry of Transport and Civil Aviation. Tarmac Civil Engineering Ltd was contracted to provide the 2¾ mile diversion of the A23 London–Brighton road and the subsidiary roadworks, and the Crawley Demolition Co. was tasked with the demolition of seventeen houses and with ground clearance for the southern runway.

At the end of 1955 demolition work was started, and Compulsory Purchase Orders were issued for the land not already acquired by agreement, including the former clubhouse of the Surrey Aero Club, which had by then become a mushroom farm. Compensation of £350,000 was agreed with Airports Ltd, which was subsequently taken over by property developers. The first meeting of the Gatwick Airport Consultative Committee was held on 17 January 1956.

Avro Anson *G-AHNT* at Gatwick in 1955. (Peter Fitzmaurice via Bill Teasdale)

Gatwick Racecourse was purchased by the MTCA that year for £248,850, and on 31 March 1956 the airfield was closed to all air movements except for the helicopters of BEA to allow development work to commence.

The main civil engineering contract was awarded to Sir Alfred McAlpine & Sons Ltd, for the construction of the runway across the site of the former racecourse. The River Mole was again diverted, this time being culverted beneath the runway. Turriff Construction Corporation Ltd received the contract for the new terminal building. The work of rebuilding the racecourse railway station alongside the terminal building went to J. Longley & Co. Ltd, who had built the original station in 1891, and the contract for the new control tower was awarded to Gilbert Ash Ltd. The consulting engineers for the new terminal building were Frederick S. Snow and Partners.

In July 1957 the Joint Parliamentary Secretary to the MTCA, Mr Airey Neave, visited the work at Gatwick and afterwards gave the press a progress report. Work on the new terminal building was well advanced, the skeleton of the runway and taxi track had been laid, and the control tower was largely complete. On 1 August the London–Brighton main road was scheduled to be diverted under the terminal building. The revised cost of the development to a single-runway layout was to be in the region of £6.8 million, including £420,000 for telecommunications and navigation equipment and radar. It was estimated that Gatwick would be usable on up to 55 per cent of the occasions when London Airport was below its weather minima, and would be able to accept diverted aircraft of the Boeing 707/DC-8 size at their landing weight.

BEA were expecting to use Gatwick for their Channel Islands and shorter Continental European services when the airport became operational in 1958. However, as of July 1957 the only independent airline to have commenced construction of new headquarters facilities at Gatwick was the UK operator Transair. This airline had been in existence since February 1947 and had previously been based at Croydon Airport. In 1957 Transair supplemented its fleet of Dakotas with two Viscount turbo-prop airliners. These could not be operated out of Croydon, and so a new hangar was planned at Gatwick, complete with a special Viscount maintenance 'dock', a series of retractable pits which were positioned underneath the undercarriage units of the aircraft. Work began on the £250,000 base early that year. In May 1958 the airline began to move in, and by June of that year all of their aircraft and some 400 staff had transferred to their new premises.

On 28 May 1958 the new Gatwick Airport Railway Station opened, on the site of the former Gatwick Racecourse Station. During June 1957 a meeting had been held to discuss the options for Croydon Airport, which was now too small for the latest airliner types. Housing had been built close by, and the residents were not happy about having a major airport on their doorstep. One suggestion was to turn Croydon Airport into a museum once Gatwick was completed and operational. However Sammy Morton, of Morton Air Services, based at Croydon at the time, was far from happy about this prospect, and said:

> The use of Gatwick as an alternative was impractical, there were 64,000 aircraft movements at Croydon last year, and they won't all be accommodated at Gatwick, it will be found to be too small. In reality, only a runway was being offered at Gatwick. For operators like himself it would cost at least £200,000 before he could put a single man in a hangar, aircraft on the tarmac, or girl in an office.

However, despite Mr Morton's dislike of Gatwick at that time, his airline duly moved in on the closure of Croydon Airport.

Transglobe Airways Canadair CL-44 G-AWGS is towed through a rather deserted Gatwick apron on 19 July 1968. Just over four months later Transglobe ceased operations. (Author's collection)

Belgian International Air Services Douglas DC-6B OO-ABE on the rain-soaked Gatwick apron on 20 May 1967. BIAS continued to operate DC-6Bs until the end of 1971. (Author's collection)

Fairey Surveys Ltd Dakota G-AHCT on a sunny day in the summer of 1967. To the right in the background can be seen the General Aviation Terminal which was opened on 1 April 1966. (Author's collection)

Caledonian Airways BAC One-Eleven series 500 G-AWWX taxis in on 26 July 1969. In the background is an Overseas National Airways DC-8, a Boeing 707, and a Convair 990. (Author's collection)

Dan-Air BAC One-Eleven G-ATPJ on its stand in the late 1960s. Work on the terminal complex continues in the background. (Author's collection)

Douglas DC-6B F-BGOB of the French charter airline Aeromaritime at Gatwick on 8 July 1967. (Author's collection)

Douglas DC-6B OH-KDC of the Finnish charter operator Kar-Air is handled by Dan-Air during its visit to Gatwick in the summer of 1969. (Author's collection)

A head-on view of Overseas National Airways Douglas DC-8 N864F, taken from the spectators' balcony on 26 July 1969. (Author's collection)

Overseas National Airways Douglas DC-8 N864F is handled by British United Airways on arrival on 26 July 1969. (Author's collection)

Douglas DC-6Bs were regular visitors to Gatwick in the late 1960s. Here, OH-KDC of the Finnish airline Kar-Air awaits passengers in the summer of 1969. (Author's collection)

Douglas DC-6B YU-AFE of the Yugoslavian charter company Adria Airways at Gatwick in the summer of 1969. (Author's collection)

Light aircraft were well catered for at Gatwick in the late 1960s. Miles Gemini G-AMDE sits outside the General Aviation Terminal on 8 July 1967. (Author's collection)

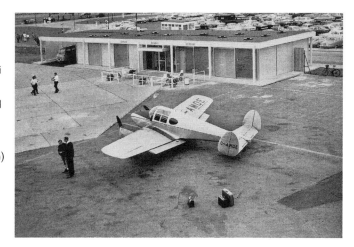

De Havilland Chipmunk G-APSB and an assortment of Piper light aircraft on the general aviation parking apron on 26 July 1969. (Author's collection)

Canadian-registered Dassault Falcon 20 executive jet CF-DML on the general aviation ramp on 19 July 1968. (Author's collection)

Douglas DC-6B I-DIMP of the Alitalia charter subsidiary SAM arrives on its stand on 8 July 1967. (Author's collection)

Douglas DC-7C EC-BDL of the Spanish charter airline Spantax taxis in on 26 July 1969. (Author's collection)

Aircraft of the Spanish airline Spantax were frequent visitors to Gatwick in the 1960s. Here, DC-7C EC-BDL manoeuvres on to its stand on 26 July 1969. (via author)

Spantax DC-7C EC-BDL, newly arrived at Gatwick on yet another holiday charter flight on 26 July 1969. (Author's collection)

Douglas DC-7C of the Spanish airline Spantax awaits another load of holidaymakers on 8 July 1967. Behind it is an Ilyushin IL-18 turbo-prop of the Romanian airline TAROM. (Author's collection)

Morton Air Services de Havilland Heron G-ANSZ sits on a lonely Gatwick apron in the late 1960s. (Author's collection)

Canadair Argonaut G-ALHI of Air Links (later to become Transglobe Airways) at Gatwick. (Air-Britain)

Morton Air Services Dakota G-AMYJ is loaded with cargo on 13 May 1967. (Author's collection)

Lloyd International Airways Bristol Britannia G-AOVP at Gatwick in the late 1960s. In the background are a British United Airways Viscount and a Boeing 707. (Author's collection)

Dan-Air Airspeed
Ambassador
G-AMAH starts
up on 26 July 1969.
(Author's collection)

A peaceful Gatwick
scene with Dan-
Air Airspeed
Ambassador
G-ALZY at rest
on 8 July 1967.
(Author's collection)

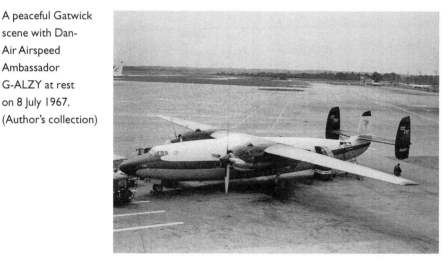

Dan-Air Airspeed
Ambassador
G-ALZN on a very
quiet Gatwick apron
on 8 July 1967.
(Author's collection)

Morton Air Services Dakota G-AOUD on its stand on 8 July 1967. (Author's collection)

French-registered Dassault Falcon 20 executive jet F-BPIO outside the General Aviation Terminal on 26 July 1969. (Author's collection)

French-registered HS-125 executive jet F-BPMC outside the General Aviation Terminal on 26 July 1969. (Author's collection)

Dan-Air Dakota G-AMSS lazes in the Gatwick sunshine during the summer of 1967. (Author's collection)

An Air London publicity shot of one of their Beagle 206 air-taxi aircraft, with British United Airways BAC One-Elevens and the Gatwick terminal behind. (Author's collection)

Donaldson International Airways Bristol Britannia G-APNB at Gatwick. (Author's collection)

A 1975 view of the British Caledonian engineering base. The Hermes fuselage used as a cabin services training unit sits alongside the perimeter road. A BCAL Boeing 707 is outside the hangar. (British-Caledonian-A Tribute collection)

A mid-1970s view of the central pier at Gatwick. Many of the aircraft present (including two TWA Boeing 747s) normally operated into Heathrow, so presumably Gatwick was receiving weather diversions that day. (J.G. Watts & Partners via Howard Smith)

A mid-1970s shot of the central pier with many unusual visiting aircraft present, presumably weather diversions from Heathrow. (J.G. Watts & Partners via Howard Smith)

A mid-1970s view of the apron from the terminal building, showing the covered walkway to the north pier, where a Laker Airways DC-10 and a Lufthansa Boeing 737 are parked. In the foreground, more building work is in progress. (J.G. Watts & Partners via Howard Smith)

A mid-1970s aerial view of the entire airport, from the end of Runway 8. (BAA via Howard Smith)

A mid-1970s aerial view of the Gatwick terminal area and the runway, with early construction work on the road spur from the M23 motorway under way. (BAA via Howard Smith)

A mid-1970s
aerial view of the
Gatwick terminal
area complex
and the runway.
(BAA via Howard
Smith)

A mid-1970s aerial shot showing construction work in progress on the spur link from the
M23 motorway into the airport. (BAA via Howard Smith)

A mid-1970s aerial view of the Gatwick terminal complex and apron. Light aircraft are parked where the satellite terminal would later be constructed, and extensive ground-level car parks can be seen. (BAA via Howard Smith)

6

A NEW START

The official opening of the Gatwick Airport took place in June 1958, but prior to this date several aircraft movements of a non-commercial nature had taken place. On 17 April 1958 a Percival Prince of the Civil Aviation Flying Unit carried out radar calibration approaches, and just after dawn on 17 May a hazard beacon was lowered into place on a 70ft pylon on Russ Hill by a BEA S-55 helicopter, with a second helicopter being used to photograph the operation. On 20 May a Varsity aircraft carried out 'runway testing' (probably checking the Instrument Landing System), and on 29 May a Heron of the Queen's Flight landed as part of a 'dry run' for the royal opening ceremony. During that day around 100 members of the press were shown around the new facilities by the commandant, Brian Oakley.

Meanwhile, on the previous day the former Gatwick Racecourse Railway Station had re-opened as Gatwick Airport Station, with the first train arriving at 6.11 a.m., and the station at Tinsley Green was abandoned. The first commercial use of the new airport again occurred in advance of the official opening date. A Transair Viscount aircraft arrived on a trooping flight from Malta at 3.45 p.m. on 30 May 1958, using the airport instead of its usual arrival point of London Airport.

The first passenger to set foot on the new Gatwick tarmac was Mrs W.I. Morrison, the wife of a Royal Navy Lieutenant, with her 8-month-old son. She told a reporter from the *Crawley Observer* that when she learned that the flight was going to land at Gatwick she had to send some hasty telegrams to people intending to meet her. That day, another Transair Viscount made the first commercial departure from Gatwick, on an inclusive tour service to Nice for Horizon Holidays. The rest of the Transair fleet transferred to their new base at Gatwick over the course of that weekend. On 7 June Transair inaugurated a seasonal scheduled service between Gatwick and Jersey.

At 10.40 a.m. on 9 June 1958, Queen Elizabeth II and Prince Philip arrived from London Airport in de Havilland Heron XM295 of the Queen's Flight to

British United Airways Bristol Britannia G-APNB in the airline's original livery. (Air-Britain)

perform the official opening of Gatwick Airport. After touchdown the Heron taxied to a stand on the north side of the central pier. For the occasion a public enclosure had been set up on the north apron, and around 7,000 members of the public came along to watch the proceedings. The event was also broadcast live by BBC television.

Parked on the north apron were a selection of aircraft of the airlines using Gatwick, including Viscounts of BEA and Transair, a de Havilland Dove of Morton Air Services, and a Jersey Airlines Heron. Parked among them was the Chipmunk aircraft used as a personal transport by Mr Peter Masefield, the managing director of the Bristol aircraft company. At the south pier were a number of BEA 'Pionair' Dakota aircraft waiting to convey passengers to the Channel Islands, and also a BEA Bristol Sycamore helicopter.

After the queen had inspected a guard of honour of ten airline captains, a speech of welcome by Mr H. Watkinson, the Minister for Transport and Civil Aviation, was preceded by a blessing from the Bishop of Kingston. The royal couple were shown models and plans of the layout of the new airport in the restaurant overlooking the airfield before the queen made a speech in which she sympathised with those whose lives were going to be affected by the airport development, but hoped that there would be some measure of compensating advantage to local inhabitants once it was in full operation.

She also said:

My husband and I travel by air often enough to realise that without proper ground control and efficient terminal facilities, quick and safe air travel would not be possible. I have not the least doubt that the latest ideas and techniques have embodied in every department of this new airport. I am quite sure the combination of a good road and rail link with modern buildings and facilities will help make a favourable impression on visitors to this country. I am sure this airport has a great future before it.

She then unveiled a commemorative plaque and accepted a bunch of roses from the 11-year-old daughter of the Minister of Transport and Civil Aviation. The royal couple then toured more of the facilities, viewing the railway station from the footbridge before returning to the airport concourse. After passing through the immigration filter they signed a few photographs in the customs hall, then boarded cars on the apron for the drive to Crawley New Town at the conclusion of their one-hour visit to Gatwick.

The first official air service departed a few minutes after the opening ceremony. A BEA Pionair class Dakota aircraft had been chartered by Surrey County Council and conveyed dignitaries and messages of goodwill to the States of Jersey and Guernsey. BEA had already made the decision to transfer most of its London–Channel Islands services to Gatwick, and these were to account for well over half of the scheduled service passengers handled at the airport that year.

The new airport at Gatwick was the first in the world to combine air, mainline railway and trunk road access facilities under one roof. Access from the railway station was via a 70ft span footbridge over the station access road. Road access

De Havilland Heron XM296 of the Queen's Flight stands outside the new terminal building, having brought Queen Elizabeth II and Prince Philip, Duke of Edinburgh for the opening ceremony on 9 June 1958. (Author's collection)

A general view of the interior of the terminal building, around 1960. (Author's collection)

was up an elevated ramp each side to a roundabout at the terminal entrance. The terminal building measured 350ft by 130ft and comprised three storeys, plus a mezzanine floor between ground and first floor at the apron end. On the roof were two rows of columns at right angles to the central pier. These were designed to support a five-storey reinforced concrete office block, to be added at a later stage.

The central pier (or finger) was a two-storey building 880ft long by 21ft wide. It was designed with stands to accommodate eleven aircraft, with provision to be made for a further seven at additional north and south piers to be constructed later. When called for their flight, passengers descended to the mezzanine floor to go along the pier to their aircraft. The finger was partitioned vertically so that international and domestic passengers were segregated for customs purposes. The walking time from the terminal building to the far end of the finger was in the region of seven to eight minutes.

A distance of 640ft along the central pier, and elevated above its roof, was the apron controllers' room. There was an operations block to the west of the terminal, with briefing rooms, meteorology and flight information services plus a telecommunications centre. Ancillary buildings included a freight shed to the south of the terminal, plus a police station to the north. Ample provision for spectators was provided at the airport. They had access to the passenger concourse buffet and restaurant, and a viewing platform was provided on top of the complete length of the central pier.

An early 1960s aerial view of the airport, showing the road access ramp and the railway station, as well as the somewhat underused ground-level car park. (Author's collection)

There was also a ground-level grass spectators' enclosure to the north of the terminal. The 7,000ft by 150ft concrete runway 09/27 had high-speed turn-offs which could be safely negotiated at speeds of 50–60 knots on to a parallel taxiway, and Calvert-type centreline and bar approach lighting. The River Mole was carried under the runway in a 14,000ft-long culvert with walls and roof of 20in thickness. Also diverted was the Gatwick Stream between the railway and the A23 road. This was carried in a culvert under the terminal and the roads for 450yd, to meet up with the River Mole north of the airport.

An unusual feature of the airport was the siting of the control tower and adjacent fire station, which were located about half a mile along the length of the runway and almost out of sight from the terminal building. This was a concession to the possible need for the control tower to serve both the present Stage 1 of the airport and the possible Stage 2. The control tower was 85ft high. The first, third and fifth floors housed the administration offices, radar room and control and navigation rooms respectively. The second and fourth floor levels had ducted floors to service the other three floors. The telecommunications equipment was accommodated in a single storey building adjacent to the control tower. Also adjacent were the five-appliance fire station and the single storey radar tower. The estimated cost of the buildings in the control tower complex was £140,000.

In the six months following the reopening of Gatwick, there were only seventy-six diversions from London Airport and other airfields in the area. This was attributed to improved methods of landing aircraft at London Airport in poor visibility, and also to the reluctance of airlines to operate a service to London if it was likely to result in an expensive and unpopular diversion to Gatwick. Scheduled airline movements were also scarce. The only airline to establish a base at Gatwick during 1958 was Transair, which opened a new £250,000 hangar and operated a mixture of newspaper, trooping and inclusive-tour flights using Dakotas and Viscounts.

Scheduled services to the Channel Islands were provided by Jersey Airlines with de Havilland Herons, later to be supplemented by Dakotas, and also by BEA which had transferred most of its services on these routes over from London Airport. BEA now had 137 staff stationed at Gatwick to handle up to seven Pionair flights to Guernsey and twice that number to Jersey, using Pionairs and Viscounts.

In October 1958 thick fog at Heathrow brought ninety-eight diverted flights into Gatwick, and between October 1958 and March 1959 BEA staff also handled 257 BEA diversions from London Airport plus a further 230 aircraft of other operators. These included the first transatlantic flights into the airport, in the form of three Pan-American Airways Douglas DC-6Bs and a Boeing Stratocruiser at the end of 1958, and early in 1959 Gatwick handled its first Boeing 707 jet when a Pan-American example diverted in from London Airport because of adverse weather conditions. During 1958, a helicopter-approach light installation, the first of its kind in the country, was installed at Gatwick.

Operations at Gatwick were not helped by a storm on 5 September 1958 which tore off part of the roof of Transair's hangar and caused the River Mole to flood

An early 1960s view of the south finger, with Dan-Air Airspeed Ambassadors, a British United Airways Viscount, and two Douglas DC-6Bs on their stands. (Dave Thaxter)

parts of the airport buildings. By the end of the year, 186,172 passengers had used the new facilities at Gatwick. This seven-month figure was six times greater than the annual total for any previous year. An unusual non-revenue visitor to Gatwick in November 1958 was the Lockheed Electra demonstrator N7144C. This four-engined turbo-prop airliner was on a worldwide sales tour, and was handled by Transair for the two-hour-long local flights it made, carrying UK airline officials and representatives of local authorities and the press.

In February 1959 Airwork transferred the operation of its 'Safari' low-cost air service to Africa, and two of its Viscounts, to its subsidiary Transair. On 17 February 1959 THY Turkish Airlines' Viscount TC-SEV was operating a special charter flight from Ankara–London via Rome with the Turkish prime minister and a party of government officials aboard. Because of poor visibility at London Airport the flight was diverted to Gatwick, but on final approach the Viscount struck trees at Jordan's Wood, about 5km from the runway threshold, and disintegrated with the loss of five crew and nine passengers.

The first foreign-scheduled airline services from Gatwick were inaugurated on 8 June 1959 by Sudan Airways, although the airline's 'Blue Nile' services to Khartoum via Rome, Athens and Cairo were actually operated by

The cover of a British United Airways brochure extolling the advantages of using Gatwick's rail-air links. (Author's collection)

A postcard showing views of the Gatwick terminal exterior and interior plus a BEA Dakota, around 1960. (Author's collection)

Viscount aircraft leased from Airwork Ltd. The flights operated twice-weekly, with fifty-three tourist class and eight first class seats on offer.

The summer of 1959 saw the beginning of an annual series of seasonal charter flights from the USA. In the beginning, most of these did not actually terminate at Gatwick but passed through on their way to or from other European airports. The first operator of these flights was Overseas National Airways (ONA), whose Douglas DC-6 N660NA arrived from Shannon and departed to Goose Bay in Canada in May. This was the beginning of a series of charters on a roughly weekly basis, most of them arriving at Gatwick from Shannon and continuing onwards to Paris, or occasionally to Frankfurt or Amsterdam.

ONA were followed in June 1959 by Capitol Airways, who used Lockheed Constellations on similar services. Between June and September 1959 TALOA operated ten Boeing Stratocruiser services into Gatwick, four of them terminating there, with the others passing through on their way to Dublin, Paris, Frankfurt or Oslo. Also during 1959, shorter-range charter flights were operated from Gatwick by the UK independent airlines Pegasus Airlines, Derby Airways and African Air Safaris (later to be renamed simply Air Safaris).

On 1 July 1960 Airwork was absorbed into British United Airways, and on 9 May 1961 BUA were to become the first airline in the world to place an order for BAC One-Eleven short-haul 'bus-stop' jets. The closure of Blackbushe

Airport on 31 May 1960 resulted in the relocation to Gatwick of several more British charter airlines. Orion Airways operated Vickers Vikings to European destinations, as did Falcon Airways, which also used larger four-engined Hermes aircraft. Dan-Air Services also moved across from Blackbushe and acquired two small offices on the first floor of the terminal building (opposite the bar!) for their operations and administration functions. However, Dan-Air's maintenance continued to be carried out at its engineering base at Lasham in Hampshire.

One of the fastest-growing UK operators at Gatwick in 1960 was the independent airline Overseas Aviation (Channel Islands) Ltd, which by then had a fleet of five thirty-six-seat Vickers Vikings, nine ex-BOAC sixty-five-seat Argonauts and a single de Havilland Dove. The airline later added fifteen former Trans-Canada Air Lines Canadair North Stars to the fleet for a purchase price of under £300,000 including spares, but in the event only eight were to be delivered. In April 1960 Overseas had a staff of 187, including twenty-three captains and twenty-two first officers.

The airline had not had an easy time moving into Gatwick. It had originally applied to the Ministry in June 1958 for permission to build a maintenance hangar at the airport. It took eleven months and a strong letter to the Minister himself to obtain approval. It then took a further six months to conclude the lease on the land. Gatwick had no hangar accommodation of its own immediately available, and some tenants and prospective tenants of the airport were worried

Eros Airlines Vickers Viking G-AJFT sits engineless at Gatwick in 1962 after the airline had ceased operations. (Author's collection)

that taking a fifty-year Ministry site lease would bring no guarantee that the airport would remain open for even five years.

However, on 14 June 1960 the airline's new hangar was officially opened by Mr Geoffrey Ripon, Parliamentary Secretary to the Ministry of Aviation, and Overseas Aviation could transfer all of its operations over from Southend. The new £300,000 hangar was of unusual timber construction, and its 150ft span made it the largest clear span timber building in the UK at that time. On 31 July 1961 Overseas inaugurated a pioneering 'no reservations' scheduled service between Prestwick and Gatwick via Manchester, but few passengers were carried.

Overseas was running into financial difficulties, and in mid-August 1961 BP stopped supplying fuel as it was owed around £250,000. A petition for the winding up of the airline was later presented jointly by BP and Rolls-Royce, as its total debts now exceeded £500,000. On 22 August 1961 the 200 engineers employed by subsidiary Overseas Aviation Engineering (GB) Ltd stopped work and sent the parent company an ultimatum regarding their futures. On 25 August sheriff officers moved into the Gatwick hangar and took away the furniture. The airline went into liquidation and its hangar was sold to Airborne Aviation Services (Gatwick) for an undisclosed price.

Other Gatwick operators who ceased operations in 1961 included Air Safaris, Falcon Airways, Pegasus Airlines, World-Wide Aviation and Swiss Universal Air Charter. For the airport, the loss of this traffic was partly compensated for by an

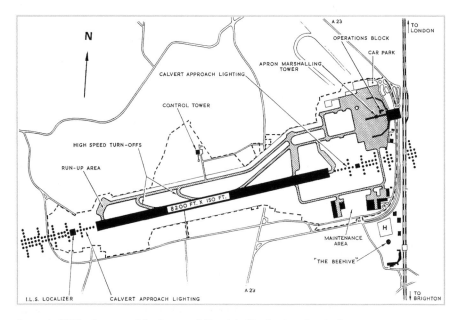

An early 1960s diagram of the layout of Gatwick. (Author's collection)

A sketch map of the
Gatwick airport layout
in 1958. (Ian Anderson)

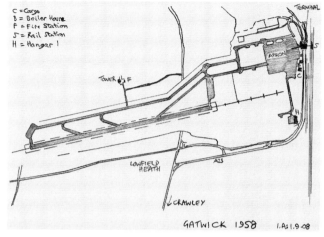

influx of transatlantic charter services by US 'supplemental' carriers. During the summers of 1960–63 these included Capitol International Airways, Flying Tiger Line, Riddle, European Asiatic, Saturn Airways and Overseas National. The aircraft used by these airlines included Douglas DC-4s, DC-6s and DC-7s, and the airport also saw services by new Spanish inclusive-tour airlines such as Aviaco and Spantax.

Another important new British charter operator at the airport was Caledonian Airways (Prestwick) Ltd, which was formed on 27 April 1961. Offices were taken at Imperial Buildings in Horley, near Gatwick, and on 15 November the airline's first aircraft, a Douglas DC-7C on lease from the Belgian airline SABENA, arrived at Gatwick. Caledonian's first revenue service was a flight on 29 November, bringing ninety-five West Indian immigrants into Gatwick from Barbados.

In April 1961 BEA introduced a new Gatwick–Paris scheduled service, and other routes were transferred across from Heathrow, but they were to prove short-lived. In December of that year BEA announced that it would no longer be serving Paris from Gatwick (nor would Air France, who had also shifted some services to the airport as part of the deal). BEA said that traffic had not come up to expectations. It had originally planned to operate four Viscount services each day, but in the event had only operated one daily round-trip. Out of the 11,000 seats offered between April and October, less than 3,000 had been sold.

British United Airways was rapidly expanding and quickly built up a large volume of inclusive-tour services and a programme of Viscount trooping flights to Germany. In 1962 the airline opened a new London town terminal at Victoria Station in conjunction with British Rail. This incorporated check-in facilities above the platform for Gatwick. During 1960 Dan-Air opened a Gatwick–Jersey scheduled service with Airspeed Ambassador aircraft and also used the type on holiday charters to Amsterdam, Brussels, Paris (Le Bourget), Munich, Nice, Santander, Tarbes and Tours. The fleet in the 1960s also included Dakotas, De Havilland Doves, Bristol 170s and Avro Yorks.

Following the closure of Croydon Airport on 30 September 1959, the long-established operator Morton Air Services had transferred its operating base to Gatwick and operated its first service into there from Rotterdam that evening using a Dove aircraft. A Gatwick–Swansea scheduled service was inaugurated a week or so later, and a large fleet of de Havilland Doves and Herons was soon being cared for at Morton's maintenance base at Gatwick. On 1 July 1960 Morton Air Services became part of the British United Airways group, but for the time being its services continued to operate under the original name.

During 1961 Air Couriers, which had been formed in 1938 at Croydon, acquired a fifty-year building lease on land in the Gatwick maintenance area and began construction of a substantial engineering base. This opened in 1962 and Air Couriers went on to specialise in third-party aircraft maintenance for airlines and corporate owners, although the company also operated a Piper Apache aircraft on training and charter flights from Gatwick for a while. On 20 January 1961 British United Airways confirmed that they would be investing £585,000 in a new hangar and offices at Gatwick.

From January 1962 Jersey Airlines began to take delivery of a fleet of Handley Page Herald turbo-prop aircraft. As well as taking over most of the schedules to the

An aerial view of the airport in August 1961. Of note is the ground-level car park and the collection of aircraft lined up on the south side. (Hans de Ridder)

An aerial view of the engineering bases in the 1960s, with the A23 road separating the British United Airways hangars from the BEA helicopter base on the other side. (Hans de Ridder)

Channel Islands, from September 1962 they were also utilised on inclusive-tour flights to the Mediterranean for tour operators Lord Brothers. On 1 May 1962 British United Airways inaugurated an all-tourist-class midweek night Viscount service from Gatwick to Malaga. This coincided with the opening to passengers of the airline's Central London Air Terminal at Victoria Station.

In April 1962 a new UK charter carrier, Eros Airlines, began operations out of Gatwick, using three Viking aircraft purchased from the liquidator of Air Safaris. Offices were made available to the airline by the Ministry of Aviation, one in the main terminal building and one (the former Falcon Airways office) in the southern finger.

However, by the end of June that year the airline's chief pilot was expressing his disillusionment with the Ministry, which he accused of 'handicapping the industry it was set up to serve'. He thought that restrictions imposed by the Air Transport Licensing Board and the Ministry were the reasons why Gatwick was currently losing £1 million a year. He claimed that the airport was used more by foreign airlines than by British carriers and that more British tourists than ever before were travelling in foreign aircraft. Preferential treatment was given to foreign aircraft at Gatwick, even though they did not use the airport during the unprofitable months.

British United Airways BAC One-Eleven G-ASJI in the airline's original livery in the early 1960s. (Hans de Ridder)

Eros had been denied passenger handling facilities of their own, and had been obliged to contract this activity out to Dan-Air. The Ministry would not grant Eros clearance to operate ad hoc charter flights between the hours of 9 a.m. and 11 a.m. on Saturdays and Sundays, and the airline was being charged £21 7s 0d (£21.35) in fees for one take off, one landing and one night's aircraft parking. Plans to purchase modern turbo-prop aircraft did not materialise, and Eros Airlines ceased trading in April 1964.

Winters at Gatwick in the early 1960s were still quiet times, and on Saturday, 15 December 1962 there were just twenty-six flight arrivals:

2.26 a.m.:	British United Airways Britannia diversion on three engines after take off from Stansted for Istanbul
3.35 a.m.:	British United Airways Viscount from Paris (Le Bourget)
6.44 a.m.:	British United Airways DC-6A from Paris (Le Bourget)
7.59 a.m.:	Privately owned Auster from Fairoaks (went onwards to Rotterdam)
10.10 a.m.:	Jersey Airlines Herald from Jersey
10.33 a.m.:	Jersey Airlines Heron from Alderney
10.44 a.m.:	British United Airways Britannia from Nice
10.57 a.m.:	Morton Air Services Dakoter from Hanover
11.50 a.m.:	Morton Air Services Dakota from Maastricht
12.25 p.m.:	British United Airways Viscount from Gutersloh

12.51 p.m.:   British United Airways Viscount from Rotterdam
1.15 p.m.:   British United Airways Britannia positioning flight from Stansted
                to pick up passengers from the earlier diverted flight
1.55 p.m.:   BEA Viscount from Guernsey
2.54 p.m.:   Jersey Airlines Herald from Radlett after maintenance
3.46 p.m.:   Morton Air Services Dakota from Jersey
4.27 p.m.:   Morton Air Services Dove on training flight
4.30 p.m.:   British United Airways Viscount from Gutersloh
4.35 p.m.:   British United Airways Viscount from Manchester
5.36 p.m.:   British United Airways Viscount from Gutersloh
5.41 p.m.:   Jersey Airlines Herald from Rome
6.08 p.m.:   British United Airways Viscount from Manchester
6.17 p.m.:   Jersey Airlines Herald from Guernsey
6.20 p.m.:   British United Airways Viscount from Gutersloh
6.24 p.m.:   British United Airways Viscount from Malaga
9.30 p.m.:   Jersey Airlines Dakota from Jersey
9.41 p.m.:   British United Airways Viscount from Tangier

The four flights from Gutersloh were part of a large trooping contract held by BUA.

In 1962 Scillonian Air Services was formed to provide an air link between London and the Isles of Scilly. Rather surprisingly, the type of equipment chosen was an Aero Commander 500A twin-engined executive aircraft. Scheduled services from Gatwick were inaugurated from Gatwick on 14 September 1963. Three flights in each direction were offered on Mondays, Wednesdays and Saturdays, but the service was not a commercial success and operations ceased on 10 October 1964.

The Civil Aviation (Licensing) Bill of 1960 had ended the state airlines' (BEA and BOAC) monopoly on scheduled services from the UK, and in theory gave independent airlines such as British United Airways equal licensing status. As a consequence, in early 1961 BUA had applied to the Air Transport Licensing Board for an extensive network of international and domestic scheduled services, mainly from Gatwick.

During 1962 work commenced on the implementation of stage 2 of the development of Gatwick. This was to include the doubling of the size of the terminal building and the addition of two more piers, but not the construction of a second runway. The north and central piers were intended for the use of international passengers only, while the south pier would handle both domestic and international services.

On 1 April 1963 Derby Airways inaugurated a service from Carlisle to Gatwick, but this was not exactly the success they were hoping for. During its first week

The fuselage of Handley Page Hermes G-ALDG, in use as a cabin services trainer by British United Airways in the 1960s. It was later used by British Caledonian Airways for the same purpose, and is now preserved at Duxford Airfield. (Ken Honey)

no passengers at all were carried. Only twenty were carried during the following week, and the service was withdrawn the following month. On 25 June 1963 the Minister of Aviation, Mr Julian Amery, spoke about the extensions at Gatwick. He estimated that they would bring the total cost of the airport up to £10,250,000. He urged the press to think of Gatwick not as a 'bucket and spade' airport, but as an extra east–west runway for Heathrow. He said that one of the objects of the runway extension was to enable the airport to accept all the types of big jets to use it, both for scheduled services and for diversions.

However, a spokesman for British United Airways maintained that their VC-10s could comfortably use the runway even without the extension. As the airport's major operator, British United accounted for 800,000 of Gatwick's 1 million passengers in 1962. Mr Amery projected that Gatwick's passenger total should rise from 1 million in 1962 to 2½ million by 1970 and to 5 million 'well before' 1980.

During 1963 British United Airways transferred the air portion of its low-cost 'Silver Arrow' London–Paris rail-air service from Lydd Airport in Kent to Gatwick. Disaster was narrowly averted on 2 September 1963 when Iberia Super Constellation EC-AMQ, on lease to the Spanish charter airline Aviaco, brushed trees on Russ Hill, about 1.75nm from the threshold of Gatwick's runway, while inbound from Barcelona. The aircraft sustained minor damage but none of the seventy-five passengers were injured.

Gatwick was still welcoming light aircraft but I was also seeing visits by the new generation of business jets and turbo-props. During June 1964 a Lockheed JetStar operated by Cameron Iron Works of Houston, Texas, flew from Edinburgh to Gatwick in forty-three minutes at an average speed of over 600mph. The aircraft brought senior executives from the USA for a series of meetings in Europe, and during its ten-day stay in Britain it was based at Air Couriers at Gatwick, who also looked after the company's Beech Super H18 aircraft.

MOVING INTO THE BIG TIME

In 1964 the existing runway was extended to 8,200ft in length in order to accept the growing number of jet aircraft movements. The concourse in the terminal building was enlarged, and on 22 June 1965 the Minister of Aviation, Mr Roy Jenkins, officially opened the new facilities. In his speech Mr Jenkins insisted that Gatwick was not a 'white elephant'. It had graduated to the position of London's second airport in its own right, and the government was now looking beyond just two airports for London and was preparing plans for the development of Stansted as well.

On 1 January 1964 BEA Helicopters Ltd was formed to take over and operate all the helicopters operated by BEA. In May of that year two new Sikorsky S-61N twenty-five-seater helicopters were delivered. One was placed on to a scheduled passenger service linking Penzance and the Isles of Scilly while the other was based at Gatwick for use on charter work. During 1964 new Affinity Group Charter rules governing transatlantic charter flights were introduced, leading to visits during 1965 from the Lockheed Electras and Constellations of American Flyers Airline, the first of the US 'travel club' airlines.

After the death of Sir Winston Churchill in 1965 there was a proposal from British United Airways (BUA) that Gatwick Airport be renamed after him, but this was not adopted. BUA continued to expand its activities throughout the mid-1960s. In October 1964 the airline's two VC-10 long-haul jets were introduced on to trooping flights from Gatwick, and the following month they were placed on to scheduled services to South America which the previous operator, BOAC, had been forced to abandon as uneconomic.

From 1965 the US charter airlines also began operating jet equipment into Gatwick, the first being a Douglas DC-8 of Capitol International in June. In July 1965 a new US operator to Gatwick arrived when Continental Airlines began Boeing 707 flights from New York, Boston, Los Angeles and Oakland. Further BUA jet services came in January 1966 when the airline operated the

An aerial view of the Gatwick terminal complex in the mid-1970s. (Author's collection)

world's first commercial service by the BAC One-Eleven 'bus stop jet' from Gatwick to Genoa on 9 April 1965.

On 4 January 1966 the One-Eleven fleet inaugurated domestic 'Interjet' services from Gatwick to Edinburgh, Glasgow and Belfast in direct competition with BEA and British Eagle flights from Heathrow. The jets were operated in a one-class seventy-four-seat configuration, and on the first day of operation 234 of the 560 seats on offer were filled, at a 42 per cent load factor. Meanwhile, the turbo-prop Viscounts of British United remained in service on inclusive-tour flights to Barcelona, Basle, Deauville, Lisbon, and other holiday destinations. In February 1966 it opened its new flight kitchens and VIP lounge at Gatwick.

In the meantime Caledonian Airways had unveiled its new blue and gold livery, when DC-7C G-ASIV arrived at Gatwick after repainting. In 1965 Airways Training was formed with its base at Gatwick. Twin Commanche and Apache aircraft were used to provide training for the twin and instrument licence ratings. Late in 1966 a subsidiary called Air London was set up to offer charter flights using Beagle 206 aircraft, and for many years these were used under contract to British United Turkeys, carrying up to 2,000 day-old turkey chicks to St Brieuc and Quimper in France.

Back in 1961 the House of Commons Select Committee on Estimates had recommended that the group of airports in the London catchment area should be removed from the control of the Ministry of Aviation and placed under the care of an independent authority. This eventually led to them being grouped together under the management of the new British Airports Authority.

The inauguration day for the BAA was set at 1 April 1966, and on this day its chairman, Mr Peter Masefield, and a party of officials and journalists toured the BAA airports by air. The tour began at Gatwick, where the official unfurling of the new (temporary) standard took place on the central pier at 11 a.m. After speeches the party departed for Heathrow aboard a chartered HS 748 turbo-prop aircraft of Channel Airways, but not before Mr Masefield had officially opened a new General Aviation Terminal to the north of the main terminal, using a golden key. At that time small aircraft engaged on business and private flights accounted for 25 per cent of Gatwick's movements.

On the same date Kingdom of Libya Airlines inaugurated a new scheduled service between Tripoli and Gatwick. Following the take over of the airport by the BAA and its rebranding as Gatwick Airport – London, a newspaper advertising campaign was mounted and the airport's general manager embarked on a tour of Europe and North America to promote the airport and bring in more airlines. During the year new services (from Bucharest by Tarom Roumanian Airlines and from Kabul by the Afghan airline Ariana) were inaugurated.

Also that year, the small UK independent British Westpoint Airlines proposed the introduction of a Gatwick–Heathrow air link, but this was not proceeded

A mid-1970s night-time shot of the central finger including (from front) a British Caledonian BAC One-Eleven, an International Caribbean Airways Boeing 707, two British Airtours Boeing 707s, a Dan-Air Comet 4B and a British Caledonian Boeing 707. (Dave Thaxter)

with, at least not for the time being. Another new operator from Gatwick in 1966 was Laker Airways, formed by the former Managing Director of British United Airways, Mr Freddie Laker. The airline commenced operations with two ex-BOAC Britannia turbo-prop aircraft, but had three One-Eleven jets on order for inclusive-tour services.

During the summer of 1966 Swissair, in co-operation with Scandinavian Air Services and Iberia, operated night-time road links by coach between Heathrow and Gatwick. This was the benefit of connecting air passengers who were flying into Heathrow on domestic and Irish services and travelling onwards on their low-fare night services from Gatwick. Meanwhile, Dan-Air Services had acquired a Piper Apache executive aircraft for use as a crew ferry and for training. On 1 September 1966 this aircraft took off from Gatwick for the short trip to Dan-Air's engineering base at Lasham in Hampshire, but struck a hill near Dunsfold and crashed with the loss of both pilots aboard.

During July and August 1966 British United Airways' engineering staff at Gatwick

Your Guide to and from the New Gatwick

The cover of a 1975 British Airports Authority guide to the surface links to Gatwick, showing the railway station, car access ramps and terminal buildings. (BAA)

started repainting the airline's fleet into a new sandstone and blue colour scheme. The new livery was applied by 'Buster' Brown and his team, which included three painters and seven assistants. They could complete the repaint of a VC-10 aircraft in seven days, using thirty gallons of paint.

In March 1967 BEA Helicopters had four Sikorsky S-61Ns in service, and had options on four more. These were intended for use on proposed services between Heathrow and Waterloo in London, which, if approved, would commence in mid-1968 and be extended later to take in Gatwick and London's still-to-be-decided third airport.

In April 1967 the expanding UK independent carrier Transglobe Airways (formerly known as Air Links) signed a contract with the US cargo airline Seaboard World for the lease of six Canadair CL-44 turbo-prop airliners, with an option to purchase at a later date. Although designed as freighters, these aircraft were to be used mainly on high density, low-cost North Atlantic passenger charters. In August 1967 it was announced that the aircraft maintenance company Air Couriers (Gatwick) Ltd had been

Air Malawi Scheduled services from Gatwick to Blantyre and regional services around East Africa.

Britannia Charter airline owned by the Thomson Organisation for its holiday company.

British Airtours The charter operation of British Airways, with its own aircraft and staff based at Gatwick.

British Caledonian Airways The UK's major independent airline and Gatwick's major operator flying most of the scheduled flights and many of the charter operations.

British Island Airways Short haul scheduled cargo and passenger operations around the UK and to places in Western Europe.

British Midland Airways Short and medium haul scheduled flights as well as charter and inclusive tour work.

Dan Air Services Wide ranging scheduled links between many UK towns and the Continent. Heavy involvement in charter and inclusive tour operations.

Laker Airways Contract inclusive tour and charter operations based on Gatwick. Operates three DC 10's, the largest aircraft based at Gatwick. Owns International Caribbean Airways.

NLM A subsidiary of KLM – Royal Dutch Airlines operating a link between Gatwick and Eindhoven.

ONA American airline operating charter flights into Gatwick from the USA.

SAM The charter side of Alitalia, the Italian national airline takes inclusive tours into Gatwick from Italy.

Wardair Canadian all charter operation using 747's and 707's between Gatwick and Canada

World Airways Californian based cargo and passenger operations, the largest of the US charter airlines.

Details and tail logos of the airlines providing regular scheduled and charter flights from Gatwick in 1975. (BAA)

Caledonian Airways Douglas DC-7C G-AOIE being towed on to its stand. (Author's collection)

acquired by Transglobe Airways for the sum of £500,000. The assets taken over included a four-bay hangar at Gatwick and a two-storey office block on the south side of the airport, and the largest tenant at the time was Laker Airways, which was renting two hangar bays and office space.

Transglobe had taken over Air Couriers in order to provide a secure base for the airline, and applied for planning permission for a hangar extension to accommodate the CL-44s, which were due to arrive in the spring of 1968. During the financial year 1967–68 Gatwick's passenger total exceeded 2 million for the first time, and a new five-storey administration block on top of the terminal building was constructed as part of Stage 3 of the development of the airport.

During 1967 the frequency of the rail services to London was increased to four semi-fast trains per hour during the busiest six months of the year. A Green Line coach link between Gatwick, Heathrow and Luton airports was also introduced.

The mid-1960s were a noisy time for the residents of the villages near Gatwick. There were many night-time departures scheduled, especially at summer weekends, and these were operated by noisy non-fan jets, supplemented by turbo-props and even the odd piston-engined airliner. Departures on 3/4 June 1967, a typical Saturday night, were as follows:

10.10 p.m.: British United Airways One-Eleven charter to Barcelona
10.44 p.m.: Dan-Air Comet 4 charter to Valencia
10.52 p.m.: British United Airways One-Eleven charter to Palma
11.35 p.m.: Laker Airways Britannia charter to Nicosia

11.39 p.m.: British United Airways VC-10 scheduled service to Entebbe
12.01 a.m.: Spantax DC-7C charter to Palma
12.06 a.m.: SAM DC-6B charter to Rome
12.09 a.m.: British United Airways One-Eleven charter to Valencia
12.12 a.m.: Transglobe Airways Britannia charter to Ibiza
12.17 a.m.: Caledonian Airways Britannia charter to Ibiza
12.21 a.m.: British United Airways One-Eleven charter to Ibiza
12.38 a.m.: British United Airways One-Eleven charter to Barcelona
1.11 a.m.: Laker Airways One-Eleven charter to Dubrovnik
1.13 a.m.: Spantax DC-7C charter to Palma
1.26 a.m.: Bavaria Flug Herald charter to Munich
1.44 a.m.: Transglobe Airways Britannia charter to Palma
1.47 a.m.: Caledonian Airways Britannia charter to Rimini
1.52 a.m.: British United Airways One-Eleven charter to Genoa
2.06 a.m.: Dan-Air Comet 4 charter to Rimini
2.19 a.m.: Swissair DC-9 flight to Zurich
2.23 a.m.: British United Airways Britannia charter to Dubrovnik
2.27 a.m.: British United Airways One-Eleven charter to Rimini
2.51 a.m.: British United Airways One-Eleven charter to Rimini
2.53 a.m.: Bavaria Flug Herald charter to Munich
2.55 a.m.: Iberia Caravelle flight to Valencia
3.04 a.m.: Transglobe Airways Britannia charter to Venice
3.16 a.m.: Iberia Caravelle charter to Barcelona
3.39 a.m.: Swissair Caravelle flight to Zurich
3.46 a.m.: Morton Air Services Dove charter to Perpignan
3.52 a.m.: Private Aero Commander flight to Munich
3.58 a.m.: Scandinavian Airlines System Caravelle flight to Bergen
4.12 a.m.: British United Airways One-Eleven charter to Basle
4.13 a.m.: Private Cessna 172 flight to Black Bourton
4.25 a.m.: British United Airways One-Eleven positioning flight to Manston
4.33 a.m.: Swissair Caravelle flight to Basle
4.43 a.m.: Swissair Caravelle flight to Zurich
4.56 a.m.: Morton Air Services Dakota freight charter to Guernsey
5.14 a.m.: Laker Airways One-Eleven charter to Ibiza
5.20 a.m.: Morton Air Services Dakota freight charter to Guernsey
5.22 a.m.: Air Spain Britannia charter to Palma
5.27 a.m.: British United Airways Viscount freight charter to Jersey
5.31 a.m.: Morton Air Services Dakota freight charter to Guernsey

In September 1967 a traffic survey conducted for the British Airports Authority showed that 62 per cent of the passengers departing from Gatwick came from within a 40-mile radius of Central London on a peak-season weekday, rising to 75 per cent on a peak-season Sunday. However, the airport's passenger catchment area was wider than that of Heathrow in terms of the proportion of passengers originating outside of the London metropolitan region – 38 per cent against 20 per cent – and most of these were from the south east.

The success of Gatwick in drawing passengers from London was credited to the airport's rail link with Victoria. Gatwick's large proportion of holiday traffic contributed to the extreme peaking of its traffic, and therefore to the annual deficit (£102,023 in 1966/67). However, the BAA Chairman, Mr Peter Masefield, had said that he expected Gatwick to become profitable in about two or three years' time.

During 1968, following a major reorganisation, the headquarters of British United Airways was transferred from Portland House in London to Gatwick. For many years British United had been applying for charter rights to the USA, and on 1 May 1968 the airline's first transatlantic charter service was operated from Gatwick to New York by a VC-10. Following previous modifications to BUA's hangar 2, extension works to hangar 3 were completed in July 1968, allowing all three of the airline's VC-10s to be housed under one roof if necessary. The scheme had cost £200,000.

On 15 September 1968 Gatwick Airport was closed for the day. Torrential rain had left the runways awash, and more rain later in the day closed many

The cover of a British Caledonian Airways brochure emphasising the convenience of the rail links from Gatwick to London and the rest of the UK. (Author's collection)

of the surrounding roads. BUA's hangar 1 was flooded, including the Special Projects Offices and the Medical Centre. Many staff were confined to the airport by road closures and had to sleep there before reporting for their next shift.

On 12 November 1968 Gatwick acquired its first transatlantic scheduled passenger service. This was not operated by Transglobe Airways as was expected, but by the Icelandic airline Loftleidir, which transferred its low-cost service to the USA via Iceland across from Heathrow. Transglobe had taken delivery of four CL-44 turbo-prop aircraft by this time, but the competition from jet-equipped rivals proved too much, and on 28 November 1968 the airline ceased operations. In all, 350 staff lost their jobs, the maintenance base at Gatwick was closed down, and around 5,000 passengers had to be found seats on alternative airlines.

The year 1969 started with another disastrous crash on the approach to Gatwick. A Boeing 727 of Ariana Afghan Airlines was operating the last leg of scheduled service flight 701 from Frankfurt to Gatwick on 5 January with sixty-two people on board when it struck trees and a house on final approach and crashed at Fernhill near Horley in poor visibility, with the loss of forty-eight lives.

In the late 1960s Dan-Air was looking for ways to reduce its overheads. One way was to outsource its ground handling services at Gatwick to an outside operator, and so a contract was awarded to Airbourne Aviation, which was owned by Mr Herbert Snowball. In order to keep pace with Dan-Air's expansion, and to be able to take on more third-party business at Gatwick, Mr Herbert Snowball entered into a partnership with Messrs Metcalfe and Foulkes to form a new company called Gatwick Handling. However, poor trading results forced this company into liquidation within a short space of time, putting Dan-Air and its other users in a difficult position.

BEA Viscount G-AOHT at Gatwick on a Channel Islands service on 26 July 1969. A British United Airways BAC One-Eleven can be seen in the background. (Author's collection)

To secure the use of the check-in desks it had contracted for, and to minimise confusion to its passengers (who had already been advised to check-in with Gatwick Handling), Dan-Air's parent company Davies and Newman came to an agreement with the failed company's creditors and the British Airports Authority that Dan-Air would still use the Gatwick Handling name for its ground handling operations in return for settling the outstanding debts. Dan-Air's need for additional check-in facilities at Gatwick led to discussions with Caledonian Airways about forming a joint ground handling company, but Caledonian's take over of British United Airways put an end to such a possibility. Instead, in February 1972 Dan-Air signed an agreement with Laker Airways, and the reorganised Gatwick Handling was awarded a ground handling concession valid for ten years.

Between April and June 1969 British United Airways placed into service its first One-Eleven series 500 jet. This stretched version of the aircraft had been ordered specifically for use on inclusive-tour charter flights. On 25 June 1969 a new air shuttle service between Gatwick and Heathrow was inaugurated by Newquay-based Westward Airways. A nine-seater Islander aircraft was used, and initially six flights per day in each direction were operated. The fare was £4 each way, and the air journey took less than fifteen minutes, compared to around an hour and a half by road. Passenger handling was provided by British United Island Airways and check-in at Gatwick utilised the General Aviation Terminal instead of the main terminal building, causing some confusion to both passengers and airline staff.

Very soon afterwards a feeder link with Newquay and Plymouth using the same aircraft was added in the mornings and evenings only, and later an onward connection to the Scilly Isles from Newquay came into operation. Westward Airways lost an aircraft in an accident at St Mary's in the Scillies in February 1970 and had to lease in a replacement aircraft at considerable cost, but continued to use an Islander on the Gatwick–Heathrow shuttle until mid-summer 1970. The service was never a commercial success.

During July 1970 the Islander was replaced by a chartered Cherokee 6 aircraft, but the service finally ceased on 22 August 1970. At the end of 1969 Gatwick was the departure point for the BP England–Australia Air Race. Under a handicapping system, the slowest of the seventy-seven entrants were flagged away from Gatwick on 17 December by round-the-world yachtsman Sir Francis Chichester, with the bulk of the remaining aircraft departing over the next two days.

It was expected that the entrants would reach Adelaide before Christmas, and would remain there until 2 January 1970 before continuing onwards to Sydney. Among the first aircraft away on 17 December were a Victa Airtourer and an Auster J1N. The last to set off was Tom Lampitt's Beech 99, which departed on 19 December and reached Sydney in forty-nine hours and forty-six minutes. Overall winner on the London–Adelaide section was BN Islander G-AXUD,

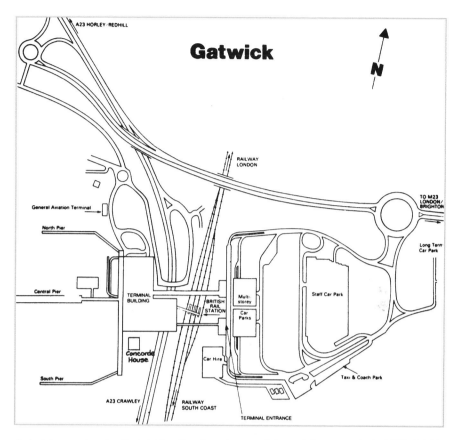

A sketch map showing Gatwick's rail and road access links and the car parks in 1977. (BAA)

which beat the handicappers to arrive in seventy-six hours and forty-one minutes after ten en route stops.

At the beginning of 1970 BEA's services from Gatwick consisted solely of flights to the Channel Islands, but in March of that year a subsidiary, BEA Airtours, commenced operations with Comet 4B aircraft acquired from the parent company. BEA Airtours had been set up in April 1969 in an attempt to take a significant share of the fast-growing inclusive-tour charter market, and was fortunate in being able to move into the recently vacated Transglobe Airways hangar accommodation at the airport.

The airline's first revenue service was operated from Gatwick to Palma on 6 March 1970 by Comet 4B G-ARJL. For the summer of 1970 nine examples were in service, and 375 staff were employed, including 111 aircrew. By the end of the year BEA Airtours was already looking around for larger aircraft to replace the Comets. The airline had its sights on the Boeing 707s offered for sale by American

Gatwick Airport
June 1976 taken from north looking south

1 Twin multi-storey car parks (under 72 hours) providing 2,000 under cover parking spaces and linked to the terminal building by a bridge. Further car parks are available for longer periods providing over 6,000 parking spaces in all. There are free coach services from remoter car parks to the airports main entrance.

2 Airport main entrance, split into two levels. Upper level for Flight Departures (drop off passengers to catch aircraft), lower level for Flight Arrivals (pick-up passengers getting off aircraft). All levels are linked by ramps and escalators.

3 Railway Station on the main London-Brighton line. There are four fast (38 mins) trains an hour to and from London, Victoria with connections all over the south east. Up to 48% of all passengers use the rail service. The station is being extensively modernised.

4 Bridge, connecting the car parks to the check-in hall, and containing Europe's widest moving walkway.

5 Second bridge with two moving walkways under construction to connect the car parks to the check-in hall and the International Arrivals Hall opened in 1977.

6 The original 1958 style terminal building which is now undergoing extensive alteration to equip it to handle International Departures and all UK Domestic flights. Completion during 1977.

7 International Arrivals Building, containing new restaurants, bars and shops as well as spacious passenger handling areas. The first parts of this building came into use in May 1974.

8 New central pier to replace the outdated 1958 style pier. It is equipped with eight moving walkways, eleven aircraft stands for wide bodied aircraft. Each stand has an air conditioned gateroom and will be served by an air jetty.

9 The runway is nearly two miles long and has handled every type of civil airliner flying, including Concorde and frequent Boeing 747's.

10 Current cargo area, to be known as Cargo Centre 2 is now totally overloaded and the new, larger Cargo Centre 1 is completed and began operations during 1977.

11 The spectators area is open daily from 08.00 until dusk. Light refreshments are available in the summer. Access is by lift from the International Arrivals Concourse.

12 Link road joining the M23 London-Brighton motorway to the A23 trunk road.

13 A23 to Crawley.

14 A23 to Redhill.

An annotated aerial view of Gatwick and its passenger facilities in June 1976. (BAA)

The former Eros Airlines Vickers Viking G-AJFT in use by the Gatwick fire service in January 1968. (Author's collection)

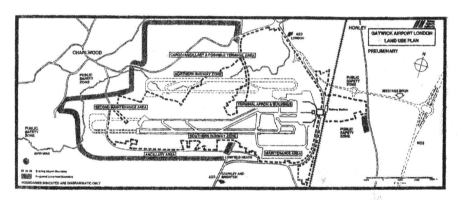

A diagram from a 1970 edition of *BUA News*, showing the plans for the proposed expansion of Gatwick by 1980. (Dave Welch)

Airlines, but was pressured by the government into purchasing aircraft from one of the state airline corporations, BEA or BOAC, and so in December 1971 the first of a fleet of seven ex-BOAC Boeing 707s arrived at Gatwick. These were converted into a 189-seat high density layout before entering service. By the 1973 summer season only five Comets were left in the fleet, and the last Comet-operated service arrived at Gatwick from Paris (Le Bourget) on 31 October 1973. On the following day the airline changed its name to British Airtours.

In March 1970 work started on new premises for the British United Airways Sports and Social Club at Gatwick. It was constructed between the old Morton Air Services hangar and the Flight Kitchens, and was named the Wingspan Club. It was formally opened (under its new name of the Caledonian/BUA Sports

An April 1978 aerial view of the southern pier at Gatwick, with British Caledonian VC-10, Boeing 707 and BAC One-Eleven aircraft clustered around it. In the background, construction work on the terminal complex continues. (Author's collection)

CP Air Douglas DC-8 CF-CPJ on a charter flight from Canada in the summer of 1976. (Author's collection)

and Social Club) on 4 December 1970. Many aviation and sports personalities attended the ceremony, including the record-breaking aviator Miss Sheila Scott. On the following day a big 'family afternoon' was held in hangar 1.

With the growth in car ownership, the proportion of passengers using the rail link to London fell to a low of 40 per cent in 1970, but rose thereafter, aided by BCAL advertisements from 1971 onwards emphasising the convenience of their

Victoria Station check-in facilities. In May 1970 the British Airports Authority published its draft plan for the future land use at Gatwick. The plan envisaged an airport capable of handling around 20 million passengers per year during the 1980s and covering an area of around 920 hectares, which was about 340 hectares more than BAA owned at the time.

A major feature of the plan was a second runway, 914m to the north of the existing runway and running parallel to it. It would have a length of 2,290m from threshold to threshold, with a 152m starter or overrun strip at either end. BAA also gave consideration to the siting of an additional 'short take-off and landing' runway to the north of the second runway. An extension to the existing aircraft parking area, and a new aircraft parking area between the two runways (enveloping the existing control tower and fire station) was also deemed necessary in order to accommodate the forecast increase in passenger numbers between 1970 and 1980, the figures from 1977 onwards including some overspill from Heathrow. The new runway was not to come about, but in 1970 the existing runway extended to 9,075ft in length to permit non-stop jet operations to the US east coast to depart with a full payload. In 1973 the runway was to be further extended to 10,165ft.

By the summer of 1970 BUA was using its stretched One-Eleven jets on a greatly expanded route network to holiday destinations such as Dubrovnik, Faro, Tenerife and Zurich. By this point, however, the airline had been in financial trouble for some time, and in late November 1970 it was taken over by Caledonian Airways. The merged airline was initially known as Caledonian/BUA.

Caravelle I-DABT of the Alitalia charter subsidiary SAM taxies in during the summer of 1972. (via author)

Gleaming Boeing 707 G-AXRS of British Caledonian Airways at their engineering base in the summer of 1977. (Author's collection)

A head-on view of Capitol International Airways Douglas DC-8 N4908C during the summer of 1972. (Author's collection)

The takeover did not include British Island Airways, which had already split off from the BUA group. In September 1971 the name was changed to British Caledonian Airways (or BCAL for short). A total of thirty-one aircraft (VC-10s, Boeing 707s and One-Elevens) and 4,400 staff were transferred to the new company, making it comparable in size to QANTAS, Air India and Aer Lingus. In mid-February 1971 the new livery of Caledonian/BUA was first displayed on One-Eleven srs 500 G-AWYS. The golden lion rampant of Caledonian was emblazoned on the tail fin, with Caledonian/BUA titles along the cabin roof.

In March 1971 the former BOAC routes from London to Lagos, Kano and Accra were transferred to Caledonian/BUA at Gatwick, and a new service to Tripoli followed on 1 July. On 1 September 1971 Caledonian/BUA formally became British Caledonian Airways Ltd, usually shortened to BCAL. On 28 January 1972 one of BCAL's VC-10 aircraft was badly damaged in a hard landing at Gatwick at the end of a short positioning flight from Heathrow and was written off. The airframe then languished at Gatwick, being cannibalised for spares until 1975 when it was finally scrapped.

Dan-Air was also expanding and in January 1971 it acquired its first Boeing 707 for use on charter flights to North America and other long-haul destinations. Dan-Air had in fact operated its first transatlantic passenger flight as far back as October 1969, when a Comet 4 aircraft flew from Port of Spain in Trinidad to Gatwick.

During 1971 affinity-group charters operated by airlines such as BCAL and Laker Airways were hit hard by spot checks at airports to check on the eligibility of passengers to travel as members of societies or other groups not specifically

Capitol International Airways Douglas DC-8 N4908C taxis in past a Dakota freighter of British Island Airways during the summer of 1972. (Author's collection)

formed for the purpose of obtaining cheap travel. On 27 March 1971 thirty-eight passengers were off-loaded from a Laker Airways Gatwick–New York flight, and two months later another flight had to leave without forty-six of its passengers after a three-and-a-half-hour delay. These passengers could not prove that they were bona-fide members of the US Left Hand Club, which had chartered the aircraft through a New York agent.

By the spring of 1971 cut-price ticket agencies were openly selling backdated society memberships along with cheap air tickets, and more and more transatlantic passengers were being interrogated at the departure airport by the Department of Trade investigators. The search for a cheap-fare alternative to the 'affinity-group' charters led to the setting up of the Laker Airways Skytrain 'walk-on' service, details of which were first announced in a press conference at the Savoy Hotel in London on 30 June 1971. In anticipation of receiving approval for the service, Laker Airways became the first airline outside of North America to acquire wide-bodied DC-10-10s when it took delivery of two examples. These were to be joined by third and fourth examples in 1974 and 1976 respectively, but had to be initially employed on various other charter services pending approval for Skytrain.

One of these charters saw the biggest-ever (at that time) uplift of passengers from Gatwick on a single flight. This took place on 21 November 1972

Aircraft of the Soviet airline Aeroflot were regular visitors to Gatwick on charter flights in the 1970s. Here, Tupolev TU-154A CCCP-85109 is on stand a Dan-Air BAC One-Eleven in the summer of 1976. (Author's collection)

A British Airtours Boeing 707 and a Dan-Air HS 748 in the summer of 1976. (via author)

when 331 passengers flew from Gatwick to Palma aboard Laker's first DC-10, which had been chartered by *Flight International* magazine. The flight was the first revenue service of a DC-10 in Europe, and around 250 of the passengers were taking advantage of an offer by the magazine's associate company Orion Travel; this included the day-trip to Majorca and back and talks by Freddie Laker and a member of the McDonnell Douglas design team for an all-inclusive price of £17.90. Meanwhile, on 9 October 1972 a Boeing 707 of the Canadian charter airline Wardair flew into Gatwick on a positioning flight from Honolulu. The 7,770 statute miles were covered in a time of thirteen hours and thirty-eight minutes, and this was believed to be the longest direct flight yet made by a 707.

In 1972 the fifteen-minute frequency of the train service to London was placed on a year-round basis. From November 1972 BCAL's remaining VC-10 aircraft were phased out and replaced by more Boeing 707s. During April 1973 work was undertaken on resurfacing the Gatwick runway. This was expected to be completed by early July and to cost some £1 million.

The work was to include the addition of a friction course to reduce the possibility of large puddles forming during heavy rain, with the consequent dangerous reduction in aircraft braking effectiveness. While the work went on the airport was closed nightly from Sunday to Thursday but remained open over the busy weekend periods. During 1973 the Soviet airline Aeroflot operated numerous charters between Gatwick and the USSR, and April was a particularly busy month in this respect. On 19 April two Tupolev TU-104 jets arrived, followed the next day by another TU-104 and an Ilyushin IL-62. Another TU-104 arrived on 22 April, and finally, on 29 April three TU-104s graced the Gatwick tarmac.

In April 1973 British Caledonian became a scheduled service operator on the North Atlantic with the inauguration of Boeing 707 schedules to New York and Los Angeles. Unfortunately, bad weather forced the inaugural New York service to divert to Boston. Until 31 March 1973 BCAL had still been using the old Caledonian Airways CA flight number prefix for its transatlantic charters, but from 1 April all flights used the BR prefix.

Later that month Boeing 707 services to Los Angeles were also introduced. In order to make these aircraft more acceptable to passengers in the 'Jumbo jet' era, five of them were fitted out internally with 'wide-bodied' look cabins, but despite this the transatlantic services were not a financial success and they were withdrawn at the end of October 1974. During the eighteen-month period of operations, over 148,000 passengers had been carried, but a loss of over £4 million had been sustained. These losses led to several European and domestic routes also being withdrawn and 800 staff were redundant, BCAL survived the crisis, unlike another Gatwick-based operator, Lloyd International Airways, which ceased operations in 1974, having operated charters with Britannia and Boeing 707 aircraft since 1969.

On 1 May 1973 KLM inaugurated Amsterdam–Gatwick services in competition with BCAL, becoming the first major non-British airline to voluntarily opt to use Gatwick. However, the Dutch carrier also continued to

Two British Caledonian Airways BAC One-Elevens on stand during the summer of 1972. (Author's collection)

Illustrating the excellent photo-opportunities available from the spectators' balcony in 1972, a view of a British Caledonian Airways BAC One-Eleven being marshalled on to its stand. (Author's collection)

serve Heathrow, and in 1974 the Gatwick service was withdrawn as an economy measure. By the summer of 1973 charter services were being operated into Gatwick by the Lufthansa subsidiary Condor using Boeing 727s, and the Finnish carrier Spearair flew Monday services with DC-8s. Pan-American Airways was also very active with transatlantic Boeing 707 charters, and during the period 8 July–11 August seventeen such flights were operated.

However, the Gatwick-based airlines were also fighting for their share of this traffic, and in September 1973 BEA Airtours won Civil Aeronautics Board and Presidential approval for charter programmes to the USA. Dan-Air was also having long-haul success, and was awarded a £1.7 million contract from CPS Jetsave for a programme of Advance Booking Charters to Vancouver, Toronto, Calgary, Trinidad and Barbados in 1974 using Boeing 707 equipment. At the time this was believed to be the largest single transatlantic charter contract to be awarded to a UK airline. By 1973 Dan-Air had become the UK's second-largest inclusive-tour passenger carrier, only beaten by Britannia Airways. The passenger figures for the Gatwick-based inclusive-tour airlines for the second quarter of 1973 were:

BEA Airtours/British Airtours: 166,847, load factor 71.8 per cent
British Caledonian: 227,837, load factor 72.9 per cent
Dan-Air: 390,827, load factor 72.7 per cent
Donaldson International: 6,786, load factor 87.3 per cent
Laker Airways: 87,356, load factor 65.5 per cent

The Decca Navigator Co's Bell 47G helicopter G-ARIA outside the Air Couriers hangar in October 1967. (Chris England)

By 1973 wide-bodied aircraft were becoming regular visitors on long-haul charters. On 12 May 1973 the inaugural World Airways Boeing 747C service from Los Angeles and Oakland carried some 420 passengers into Gatwick, and during that same month a Boeing 747 of the Canadian operator Wardair arrived from Toronto with 452 passengers aboard. From November 1973 Lockheed TriStars of Luton-based Court Line Aviation commenced holiday charter flights from Gatwick to the Caribbean.

During the following year, however, the airline and its associated tour company Clarkson Holidays collapsed. In July 1974 the BAA published its revised master plan for Gatwick, based on assumptions made in the aftermath of the 1973 world fuel crisis and the reduction in disposable income available for air travel. In order to meet a forecasted future passenger level of 16 million travellers per year, the existing central pier was scheduled to be replaced in 1977 by a new one equipped with air jetties, eight moving walkways, and gates for up to eleven wide-bodied aircraft at a time. A new link road would connect the airport with the M23 motorway.

Two multi-storey car parks for over 6,000 vehicles were already under construction, and a new northward extension to the terminal building to handle international arrivals and extensive new catering facilities were to be opened in 1975. To the north of the runway, a new maintenance area and cargo area were planned. There were no longer any plans for a second runway, despite the fact that in 1974 Gatwick was linked to fifty-seven cities around the world by some fourteen scheduled airlines. Of these the largest were BCAL, Dan-Air, KLM and British Island Airways.

The airport was also served by a large number of charter flights, the major carriers including Laker Airways, Dan-Air, Trans-International Airways, World Airways, and British Airtours. Because the name Gatwick was still associated in the minds of the travelling public with holiday charter flights there was a suggestion around this time that the airport might be renamed, either as London South Airport (with Heathrow as London West), or as Churchill International Airport, but these ideas were not adopted and London (Gatwick) it remained.

In 1975 the Gatwick Promotion Group was formed to market the airport more widely. One of its first achievements was to persuade the board of British Railways to redevelop the railway station by building a 'raft' over the platforms. This was opened in 1980. By 1975 the average rail journey time from Gatwick to Victoria Station had been reduced to thirty-eight minutes. It was the long-term aim of the Group to introduce non-stop rail services between the airport and central London, and this eventually led to the introduction of the Gatwick Express dedicated rail link. For passengers arriving by car, a new multi-storey car

Former RAF Air Support Command Avro Anson TX228 sits in the British United Airways maintenance area in March 1969, with its wings and rudder removed for road shipment to Crawley Technical College. (Chris England)

Westward Airways BN Islander outside the General Aviation Terminal in August 1969 while operating the Gatwick–Heathrow air-shuttle service. (Chris England)

park complex was opened on the east side of the station in 1975, together with a spur road linking the airport to the M23 motorway.

In 1975 Gatwick Airport Director John Mulkern announced that 'by 1978 Gatwick will be a better airport for the passenger than Heathrow'. Mr Nigel Foulkes, Chairman of the British Airports Authority, said that since the present Gatwick airport was opened in 1958 it had borne the brunt of the boom in highly seasonal charter traffic, and with its charter bias it had taken the full weight of the wide-bodied generation of aircraft. Whereas scheduled service Boeing 747s operated into Heathrow in low-density, mixed-class layouts with low load factors, Gatwick handled advance-booking and inclusive-tour charter aircraft carrying nearly 500 passengers.

Mr Foulkes said that if Gatwick was to take scheduled international traffic 'a complete transformation' was necessary. BAA was keen to impress the convenience of Gatwick on airlines and the British government, and would have liked to see airlines move voluntarily to Gatwick before saturation at Heathrow forced the issue. However, all bilateral agreements between national carriers named a specific airport, and many foreign airlines were reluctant to fly to what they saw as a 'second-line' destination while their British partners still operated out of their 'first-line' home airport.

On 20 July 1975 an incident befell British Island Airways' Herald aircraft G-APWF, which was operating a flight to Guernsey. After take off the undercarriage was retracted, but after the aircraft had travelled about 411ft it sank back on to the runway, fortunately without injury to any of its forty-five occupants.

On 3 June 1976 BCAL announced an order for two wide-bodied Douglas DC-10-30s for delivery in 1977. At that time, none of BCAL's existing hangars could completely accommodate a DC-10, although the long-haul maintenance hangar used by its Boeing 707s could accept a DC-10 apart from its tail. It was decided to add DC-10 tail-dock doors to this hangar, which would run the full 480ft width of the building. These doors would completely enclose the tail and would provide five working levels for the engineers. The doors were built by a Southampton-based company and were completed in time for the delivery of BCAL's first DC-10 on 13 March 1977.

In December 1977 BCAL announced that work was to commence on a new DC-10 hangar at Gatwick. The 3,500-squaremetre building would be completed at the end of 1979 at a cost of around £5.25 million.

On 21 July 1976 the £450,000 modernisation of accommodation and equipment for Gatwick's air traffic control and meteorological services was officially opened. The new facilities were housed in an extension to the existing air traffic control building, which had remained virtually unchanged since the opening of the redeveloped airport in 1958, despite a fourfold increase in the approach control workload.

The original plan had the approach radar suites located on a mezzanine level, adjacent to the visual control room. It was realised after the original design had been completed that the space available for the radar was inadequate, and so the approach radar was moved to a lower floor. This arrangement had worked well

Israeli Air Defence Force Boeing Stratocruiser 4X-FPX visiting Gatwick in 1970. (Mick West)

for eighteen years, but current traffic loads at Gatwick had exposed its limitations. Gatwick controllers must have welcomed the improvement in working conditions, but they still had to request heading changes from flights in order to positively identify aircraft. In order to rectify this, processed secondary radar was due to be introduced during 1977.

In November 1976 the airport's new international arrivals building and its associated car parks won an award from the Central Council for the Disabled for the quality of its provisions for disabled travellers. The arrivals building was described as 'the best building for disabled travellers to be completed in the last five years'. Elsewhere at Gatwick, modernisation work was continuing on schedule for completion in 1978/79. At the end of October 1976, the first half of the revamped check-in hall was opened. This included thirty-six check-in desks for Gatwick Handling and British Airtours, and a new computer-controlled baggage conveyor-belt system.

On the cargo side of things, the first shed in the new cargo centre was due shortly to be handed over to BCAL. Also in October 1976, British Caledonian became the British flag carrier to most of South America, following the transfer of route licences from British Airways. A Boeing 707 schedule to Caracas and Lima commenced on 26 October, with a second weekly service also calling at Bogota. During the financial year 1976/77 the airport handled 83,304 tonnes of freight. After a worldwide drop in passenger numbers caused by the oil crisis of 1974, the volume handled at Gatwick rose again to reach 5.9 million for the financial year 1976/77.

In April 1977 Trade Secretary Edmund Dell announced his government's long-awaited scheme to encourage more use of Gatwick. From 1 April 1978 no British or foreign whole-plane charters would be allowed to use Heathrow. No further expansion (such as a fourth terminal) at Heathrow would be allowed until Gatwick

British Island Airways Dakota freighter G-AMHJ swoops in to land at Gatwick. (Mick West)

Avro Anson G-AGWE of Kemps Aerial Surveys about to touch down at Gatwick in 1971. In the background are Boeing 707s. (Mick West)

Royal Canadian Air Force aircraft were regular visitors to Gatwick in the 1960s. This is C-130E Hercules 10324 in 1968. (Mick West)

was fully utilised and handling something close to its maximum 18 million passengers per year. The government's policy was based on four principles:

1. Both scheduled and charter traffic should be transferred to Gatwick.
2. Both British and foreign carriers on particular routes should move.
3. Both long-haul and short-haul traffic needed to be relocated.
4. The redistribution should be achieved through consultation rather than direction.

The government estimated that if it had not intervened, 750,000 charter passengers, mainly carried by British Airways, Pan American Airways and TWA, would have used Heathrow instead of Gatwick during 1978. It was hoped that by 1982 3–4 million passengers a year, of which charter passengers would total 1 million, would have been transferred to Gatwick.

BEA Westland WS55 Whirlwind helicopter G-AOCF fitted with pontoon floats is seen outside the BEA helicopter base during 1966. (Mick West)

A scene at the British United Airways engineering base during 1966, with former RAF Avro Anson TX228 nearest, along with BUA Viscounts and a Handley Page Herald. (Mick West)

In 1977 Pier 2 at Gatwick was opened, enabling wide-bodied aircraft to be handled in the central area. Gatwick now had fifty-five aircraft stands, twenty-four of which were capable of taking wide-bodied airliners. Many of the stands were equipped with automated parking systems which enabled pilots to position their aircraft accurately on the stand without the need for a marshaller, and some stands had a hydrant refuelling facility and fixed ground power supply, reducing

British United
Airways Handley
Page Heralds
were mainly
used on services
to the Channel
Islands. Here,
G-APWH sits
at the BUA
engineering base
in 1968. (Mick
West)

the congestion contributed to by ground vehicles. Fire cover at the airport was maintained on a twenty-four-hour basis by a total force of around seventy officers and ten fire appliances, including two rapid response vehicles.

In 1977 BCAL introduced its first two wide-bodied DC-10-30s into service. The first example, G-BEBM, entered service on 20 March on BCAL's busiest long-haul route, from Gatwick to Lagos. This aircraft was joined on 15 May by G-BEBL, initially flying on North Atlantic charter flights. At 5.35 p.m. on 26 September 1977, the long-awaited inaugural flight of the Laker Airways Skytrain 'walk-on' service to New York departed. Prospective passengers had begun queuing at Gatwick sixty-five hours before the scheduled departure time, and the eventual passenger load on the 345-seat DC-10-10 comprised 272 adults and children and three infants at a fare of £59 one way. On the return leg a full load was uplifted from New York, with the first full load out of Gatwick being carried on 2 October.

Pleased with the results of Skytrain's first week of operation, Freddie Laker signed a letter of intent for two more DC-10s and announced that from 1 April 1978 there would be fourteen Skytrain services each week, with the operations divided equally between DC-10 and Boeing 707 equipment.

For the summer of 1977 scheduled services were operated from Gatwick to a large number of destinations as follows:

Aberdeen: two daily by British Airways; Accra: three weekly by BCAL; Algiers: three weekly by BCAL; Amsterdam: up to four daily by BCAL; Banjul: two weekly by BCAL;   Barbados: four weekly by Caribbean Airways; Belfast: up to three daily by British Midland Airways; Berne: nine weekly by Dan-Air; Blackpool: one daily except Sats by BIA/BCAL; Blantyre: two weekly by Air

Lear Jet 23 HB-VAM, an early executive jet, at the British United Airways Gatwick base during 1966. (Mick West)

Luxair Lockheed L-1649A Starliner LX-LGY, used on charters from South Africa, seen at Gatwick in 1968. (Mick West)

Malawi; Bogota: one weekly by BCAL; Brussels: up to three daily by BCAL; Buenos Aires: two weekly by BCAL; Caen: ten weekly by Touraine Air Transport; Caracas: two weekly by BCAL; Casablanca: four weekly by BCAL; Colmar: one daily except Sats by Air Alsace; Clermont-Ferrand: three weekly by Dan-Air; Dakar: one weekly by BCAL; Deauville: five weekly by Lucas Air Transport; Dijon: six weekly by Air Alsace; Edinburgh: up to four daily by BCAL; Eindhoven: ten weekly by NLM; Freetown: four weekly by BCAL; Genoa: one daily except Suns by BCAL; Glasgow: up to five daily by BCAL; Guernsey: at least two daily by BIA/British Airways; Houston: one daily by BCAL; Isle of Man: up to two daily by Dan-Air/BIA; Jersey: up to seven daily by BCAL/Dan-Air; Kano: three weekly by BCAL; Kristiansand: five weekly by Dan-Air; Lagos: one daily by BCAL; Las Palmas: three weekly by BCAL; Le Havre: ten weekly by Touraine Air Transport; Le Touquet: three daily by BIA/BCAL; Lima: two weekly by BCAL;

Dan-Air's Piper Apache G-ATFZ, which was used for ferrying crews and for training, was lost in a crash near Gatwick on 1 September 1966. (Dave Welch)

A busy scene in 1966, with the Gatwick apron crowded with diversions from Heathrow, including British Eagle Viscount G-ATDR and several BEA Vanguards. (Dave Welch)

Lisbon: one weekly by BCAL; Lusaka: three weekly by BCAL; Manchester: two daily by BIA/BCAL; Maastricht: ten daily by NLM; Monrovia: two weekly by BCAL; Nancy: one daily except Sats by Air Alsace; Ndola: three weekly by BCAL; Newcastle: ten weekly by Dan-Air; Ostend: one weekly by Dan-Air; Paris: up to six daily by BCAL; Perpignan: one weekly by Dan-Air; Poitiers: five weekly by Touraine Air Transport; Recife: two weekly by BCAL; Rio de Janeiro: three weekly by BCAL; Rotterdam: up to three daily by BIA/BCAL; Rouen: ten weekly by Touraine Air Transport; Santiago (Chile): two weekly by BCAL; Sao Paulo: three weekly by BCAL; Strasbourg: two weekly by Dan-Air; Tenerife: one weekly by BCAL; Tours: five weekly by Touraine Air Transport; Tripoli: three weekly by BCAL; Tunis: two weekly by BCAL.

In July 1977 BCAL's new dedicated cargo handling facility at Gatwick came into service. It was four times larger than the airline's previous cargo terminal,

British Airways Helicopters' Bell Jet Ranger G-AWGU outside the former 'Beehive' terminal in the mid-1970s. (Mick West)

This line-up of airliners at the central finger in 1978 includes a Douglas DC-10 and Boeing 707s of British Caledonian Airways, a Delta Airlines Lockheed Tristar, a Laker Skytrain DC-10, and Boeing 747s of Braniff International and Wardair. (BAA)

and over £1 million was spent on fitting it out with the latest freight handling vehicles and equipment. By this time there were three major cargo airlines based at Gatwick, and many European shippers were transporting goods across the Channel in TIR lorries for trans-shipment on cargo flights out of the airport.

By 1977 over 80,000 tonnes annually was being processed in the limited space available in the original 1958 cargo centre, which had been designed to handle just 50,000 tonnes each year. A new facility for airlines other than British Caledonian was urgently needed, and the first phase of this was constructed to the north of the runway. The first of an eventual four transit sheds was operational. Each of these was equipped to handle the up to 100 tons of containerised cargo that could arrive on a Boeing 747 freighter. Large, slow-moving road traffic bound for the cargo centre had the exclusive use of a dedicated access route into the airport, and plans were in hand for the construction in 1978 of stands for five large aircraft in the cargo area and a taxiway for their exclusive use.

Amidst the general growth in airline traffic there was one service loss, however. On 28 February 1977 British United Air Ferries had withdrawn its Gatwick–Le Touquet car-ferry service as a result of continuing losses incurred on its car ferry network as a whole. Until Heathrow and Gatwick could be connected by a motorway road link there was a need for a fast and reliable way for transferring passengers between the two airports without going into central London, and in 1978 the Gatwick–Heathrow Airlink was set up as a joint venture between the British Airports Authority, British Airways Helicopters, and BCAL.

This used a Sikorsky S-61N helicopter, appropriately registered G-LINK, which was owned by BAA, with British Airways Helicopters providing the flight crew, engineering support and back-up aircraft, and BCAL providing the cabin crew, passenger services and other ground support. In later years British Airways

A British United Airways BAC One-Eleven and two of their Britannias, all in the new BUA livery at Gatwick in August 1967. (Chris England)

Two Dan-Air Comet 4s (G-APDK nearest) at Gatwick in October 1967. In the background is a Britannia of Caledonian Airways. (Chris England)

Helicopters was to withdraw from the joint venture, and BCAL Helicopters was to step in to take over the necessary staffing and engineering support.

The helicopter was parked overnight at Gatwick, initially at the British Airways Helicopters base at the south end of the airport, and making the short positioning 'hop' to Stand 1 at the main terminal for the first service of the day. At Heathrow it utilised Stand H34. A high degree of punctuality was achieved, thanks to good co-operation from air traffic control staff at both airports. The initial service frequency consisted of ten fifteen-minute flights daily in each direction between 7.10 a.m. and 7.30 p.m., with the cabin configured to accommodate twenty-eight passengers.

The inauguration of the helicopter link coincided with the official opening of the improved and enlarged terminal facilities at Gatwick by Charles, the Prince of Wales. On 9 June 1978, exactly twenty years after Queen Elizabeth II had

Bristol Britannia G-ATNZ of Caledonian Airways on the Gatwick apron in August 1968. (Chris England)

Dan-Air Comet 4 G-APDM, minus its outer wings, in use as the airline's cabin training unit in November 1978. (Tom Singfield)

An aerial view of the British Caledonian hangar in 1973, with a VC-10 outside. (Ian Anderson)

A British United Airways VC-10 in their VC-10 hangar in 1973. (Tom Samson via Ian Anderson)

An aerial view of the Laker Airways hangar during 1973, with a DC-10 and a Boeing 707 outside. (Ian Anderson)

The former Transair, and then British United Airways, Hangar 1 after its take over by British Airways in 1974. (Ian Anderson)

performed a similar function at the opening of the 'new' Gatwick, he arrived on the inaugural service of British Rail's Rapid City Link train service from Victoria Station, accompanied by the chairman of the British Railways Board, Sir Peter Parker. After touring the new airport facilities he departed for Heathrow on the inaugural Airlink helicopter service.

As a result of the renegotiation of the UK–USA air services agreement in 1977, several new transatlantic air services commenced in 1978. Delta Air Lines inaugurated daily Tri-Star services to Atlanta on 1 May, and they were followed shortly afterwards by Braniff International with services to Dallas/Fort Worth with its brightly painted 'Big Orange' Boeing 747 aircraft. Other new routes that year included Gatwick–Bogota services by the Colombian airline Avianca. Laker Airways expanded its Skytrain concept by adding a new route to Los Angeles in September, and new shorter-range services were inaugurated to Dublin by Aer Lingus and to Plymouth by Brymon Airways.

Dan-Air expanded its scheduled service network by adding flights to Bergen in 1978, to Dijon and Toulouse in 1979, and to Munich in 1980. During 1979 there had been complaints about British Airways' service to Aberdeen, and in November Dan-Air replaced the national carrier on the route. The French regional airline Brit Air inaugurated services from Gatwick to Le Havre, Caen, Rennes, Morlaix and Quimper in April 1979. In 1978 British Island

Transglobe Airways Bristol Britannia G-ATLE at their engineering base (formerly the Air Couriers base) in March 1968. (Chris England)

The Sikorsky S-61N helicopter G-LINK used on the Gatwick–Heathrow Airlink service, pictured in September 1978. (Chris England)

Airways purchased three One-Eleven jets in order to enter the inclusive-tour charter market.

By the mid-1970s Dan-Air had amassed a dedicated charter fleet of twenty-eight jets (Comets, One-Elevens and Boeing 727s), but these were all rather elderly aircraft whose low initial purchase price was offset by very high operating costs, especially the fuel-thirsty Comets. One tour client, the leading UK tour operator Intasun, specialised in offering cheap tours by flying in the off-peak time slots that its rivals did not want, but Dan-Air was finding it increasingly difficult to offer attractive charter rates using its ageing fleet.

Eventually, two Dan-Air executives approached Intasun with a proposal that they should leave Dan-Air and set up their own airline with new, fuel-efficient aircraft. Harry Goodman of Intasun agreed to take one-third of the new airline's seat capacity, all at off-peak times, in return for a shareholding. A deposit was paid on three brand new Boeing 737s for delivery from April 1979, and in July 1978 it was announced that Intasun had set up its own airline. The name was still to be announced, but was later revealed to be Air Europe. The year 1978 was noteworthy for scheduled airline movements exceeding those of charter flights for the first time.

Gatwick's passenger traffic rose by 18 per cent that year, but the air traveller's experience was marred by long delays on European flights caused by air traffic control difficulties. Long queues for the standby fare flights to the USA led to the erection of a marquee in the grounds of the airport to provide some basic comforts for the would-be travellers. In August 1978 British Caledonian Airways announced plans to construct a nine-storey £16 million headquarters building in Crawley, near Gatwick, to house the 1,100 office staff currently working out of smaller buildings at Gatwick. The work was completed on 30 November 1980 (St Andrew's Day).

On 23 April 1979 the Gatwick–Heathrow Airlink helicopter service carried its 50,000th passenger. The new charter carrier Air Europe operated its first revenue service on 4 May 1979 when Boeing 737 G-BMHG carried 130 passengers from Gatwick to Palma on flight KS1004. In August 1979 BAA signed a legally binding document pledging not to build a second runway for at least forty years, and in return the West Sussex County Council agreed to the upgrading of the taxiway running parallel to the runway to permit its use as an emergency landing strip in the event of the main runway becoming non-operational.

During the following month BAA outlined its plans for the expansion of Gatwick to meet the anticipated passenger demand in the 1980s. These plans included a second passenger terminal and new cargo and maintenance facilities. The new second terminal would be surrounded by some twenty aircraft stands, and would be linked to the original terminal and the railway station by a 'people mover' tracked transit system. The existing north pier was to be replaced by a satellite terminal capable of handling eight wide-bodied aircraft. These plans were to go before a public enquiry in 1980.

The year 1979 saw the commencement of a new scheduled service to Colombo operated by Air Lanka. During the following year new services were inaugurated to Manila by Philippine Airlines Boeing 747s, to St Louis and Atlanta by BCAL, and to Miami by Laker Airways Skytrain. British Rail also upgraded its rail links to the airport, adding twice-daily through services to Manchester in May 1979 and an hourly service to Reading in May 1980.

In August 1979, at a Cabinet meeting at 10 Downing Street presided over by Prime Minister Margaret Thatcher, the Secretary of State for Trade, John Nott, said that the problem of overcrowding at Heathrow was becoming acute, and he would be bringing the question of a third London airport before the Cabinet in the autumn. However, it was meanwhile essential to take steps to relieve congestion by transferring certain services from Heathrow to Gatwick. He had concluded with regret that there was no acceptable alternative to transferring most services between London and Canada and between London and Spain and Portugal.

This was to be the beginning of a long, bitter and mostly unsuccessful attempt to force airlines to switch services to Gatwick. In 1979 the Civil Aviation Authority held a public hearing into the proposed renewal of the licence for the Gatwick–Heathrow helicopter link. A spokesman for the residents of Hookwood, a village near Gatwick, said that people 'live in fear of the helicopter', and that their properties had been devalued by £5,000 because they were under the helicopter flight path. In requesting a four-year extension, BCAL said that the link was vital to the development of Gatwick and to relieving congestion at Heathrow. BCAL estimated that the link brought in extra revenue in the region of £750,000 per annum.

All-freight carrier British Cargo Airlines opened its new bonded freight terminal at the airport in 1979. The end of the 1970s saw the withdrawal of the Dan-Air Comet fleet. The airline's last Comet 4B, G-APYD, touched down at Gatwick on 23 October 1979 at the end of its final service, a holiday charter from Heraklion in Crete. A week later it was airborne from Gatwick once again for the short flight to the Science Museum's airfield at Wroughton in Wiltshire, where it was to join the museum's collection of preserved airliners. Comet 4 G-APDB had previously been flown into Duxford Airfield for preservation by the Duxford Aviation Society, but there was one more chance for enthusiasts to enjoy a flight in a Dan-Air Comet.

On 9 November 1980 Comet 4C G-BDIW took off from Gatwick on flight DA8874, a one-hour special enthusiasts' flight arranged by Ian Allan Ltd. With a full load of 119 passengers aboard, the Comet carried out low fly-bys at Heathrow, RAF Brize Norton, and RAF Lyneham before finally landing back at Gatwick. In 1980, under pressure from the government, British Airways agreed to transfer all its Iberian Peninsular services to Gatwick, starting in October of that year. Services to Spain would switch from 26 October, adding thirty-six flights per week to the airline's weekly total out of Gatwick and making it by far the largest airline based there, if British Airtours' services were included. All the flights would be operated by new Boeing 737s.

Services to Portugal would follow in the spring of 1981. However, these moves would not be matched by its Spanish and Portuguese counterparts Iberia and TAP, as they had in October 1978 obtained a High Court injunction preventing them from being forced to transfer their London flights to Gatwick. Discussions with Air Canada over a transfer of Canadian flights had been ongoing since April 1978, with Air Canada claiming that interlining facilities at Gatwick were inferior to those at Heathrow and that such a move would bring with it heavy losses, despite the UK government claiming that Air Canada would save around $2 million through lower landing fees.

In 1980 BCAL invested some £5.25 million in a 5,000m^2 hangar project on the south side of the airport, capable of handling the airline's expanding fleet of wide-bodied DC-10s. Elsewhere, work continued on upgrading the airport facilities, including the replacement of the north pier by a satellite terminal linked to the main building by an automatic rapid transit system, the first of its kind outside the USA. With its major resident airlines such as BCAL, Laker Airways, Dan-Air and British Airtours all looking forward to introducing new fleets and planning new routes, at the start of the 1980s Gatwick was preparing for yet more growth as it marked the completion of fifty years as a licensed aerodrome.

POSTSCRIPT

This book covers in some detail the fifty years up to the beginning of the 1980s, but nothing stands still, especially in the dynamic world of air transport, and since then the airport has continued to undergo significant development. In 1983 the satellite pier was officially opened, primarily to handle wide-bodied aircraft. This replaced the north pier, and was linked to the main terminal building by a driverless Westinghouse Rapid Transit System, the first application of its kind outside of the USA. However, even this was recognised as only a stop-gap solution to the airport's expanding traffic, and in that same year work commenced on the construction of a second main terminal building.

The year 1984 saw the launch of Inter City's non-stop Gatwick Express rail services to London and the official opening of a new 45m-high stalk-mounted visual control room to supercede the nearby 1950s-vintage control tower. In 1958 work commenced on a new northern runway parallel to the existing one,

A June 1983 view of the driverless railway linking the main terminal to the satellite terminal. (Author's collection)

British Airtours Boeing
737 G-BGJM taxis
past the Laker Airways
hangars in 1981.
(Author's collection)

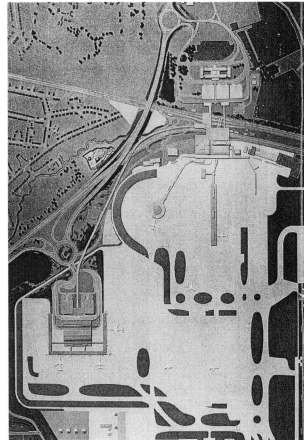

A 1980 diagram of
the layout of London
(Gatwick) terminal area,
including the proposed
satellite terminal and
second terminal building.
(BAA)

A 'first-day cover' issued in 1983 to commemorate Dan-Air's thirty years of operations. (Author's collection)

but as agreed it was only authorised to be used as a runway in emergency. Under normal conditions it was to serve as a taxiway. By then Pier 1 was the only part of the terminal complex that remained unchanged since its 1958 opening, and in 1985 a complete modernisation and refurbishment of this pier was carried out.

During the year ending April 1987 Gatwick overtook New York's John F. Kennedy International Airport to become the world's second-busiest airport in terms of international passengers, handling 15.86 million. In 1988 the new North Terminal was officially opened by Queen Elizabeth II. With the opening of this second terminal the original one was named the South Terminal. A second pier was added to the North Terminal in 1991. And so into the twenty-first century …

In 2004 a new passenger Air Bridge linking the North Terminal to Pier 6 and spanning Taxiway Lima was lifted into position over the weekend of 22/23 May, and was officially opened on 16 May 2005. In 2004 the last vestiges of the once plentiful spectators' facilities at the airport were removed with the closure of the Gatwick Skyview viewing terrace on the fourth floor of the South Terminal. As well as offering views across the airport (even though these had become increasingly restricted as more and more building work took place), and a shop/cafe, the Skyview terrace had also displayed the nose section of a Comet 1 jet and a complete Handley Page Herald turbo-prop airliner. In September 2008 the now-privatised British Airports Authority Ltd announced that Gatwick Airport was to be offered for sale, and on 4 December 2009 Global Infrastructure Partners became the new owner.

Meanwhile, what had become of Gatwick's resident airlines? Dan-Air appeared to flourish for some considerable time, and in 1983 became the first airline in the world to operate the BAe 146 regional jet airliner. The airline later acquired wide-bodied Airbus A300 aircraft, and in 1990 its subsidiary Dan-Air Engineering opened a large new hangar on the northern side of the runway. However, the airline eventually succumbed to financial problems and was purchased by British Airways in 1992 for a nominal £1. The engineering hangar was eventually taken over by FLS Aerospace in 1997.

The Sikorsky S-61N helicopter G-LINK, used on the Gatwick–Heathrow Airlink service until 1982. (Simon Shearburn)

A 1980 view of the British Caledonian and Laker Airways engineering bases, bordered by the revised road layout. The London–Brighton railway line can be seen at the bottom of the picture. (British-Caledonian-A Tribute collection)

British Airways had meanwhile also taken over British Caledonian Airways in January 1988, and British Airways engineering had moved into part of the former British United Airways maintenance facility. The Gatwick–Heathrow Airlink helicopter service ceased operations on 6 February 1982, following the completion of the M25 motorway between junctions 8 and 10. Throughout its existence it had been the target of vociferous campaigning over noise levels and low-flying. Laker Airways and its Skytrain collapsed on 5 February 1982 after a bitter price war with Pan American Airways, British Airways, and other transatlantic operators. After developing a scheduled service network, Air Europe also ceased operations on 8 March 1991.

However, new airlines sprang into being to take the place of the failed ones. One of the most high-profile and successful of these was Virgin Atlantic Airways, which operated its inaugural service from Gatwick to New York (Newark) on 22 June 1984. Low-cost carriers such as Flybe also established bases at Gatwick, and in April 2008 EasyJet became the airport's largest short-haul operator, with flights to sixty-two UK and European destinations.

APPENDIX I

BRITISH INDEPENDENT AIRLINES AT GATWICK FROM 1946–80

✧ **Ace Freighters**: Was an all-cargo airline that established a base at Gatwick in 1964 and operated its first charter flight with a Constellation aircraft on 1 March that year. A small fleet of Constellations and Douglas DC-4s was built up, but the airline ceased operations in 1966.

✧ **Air Europe**: Was a subsidiary of the International Leisure Group and commenced operations from its Gatwick base in May 1979 with three new Boeing 737s. Air Europe was the main supplier of charter seats to Intasun Leisure, which grew to be the UK's second-largest tour operator during the 1980s.

✧ **Air Safaris**: Originally named African Air Safaris, this charter airline was initially based at Southend Airport, but flew inclusive-tour services out of Gatwick with two Viking aircraft during the summer of 1959. In November 1959 it shortened its name and transferred its operating base to Gatwick. During 1960 more Vikings and a four-engined Hermes aircraft joined the fleet, but Air Safaris ceased operations on 31 October 1961.

✧ **Airwork**: This important independent airline transferred its operating base from Blackbushe Airport to Gatwick, and on 8 June 1959 it began operating the 'Blue Nile' service from Gatwick to Khartoum on behalf of Sudan Airways, using Viscount aircraft. On 1 July 1960 Airwork merged with Hunting-Clan Air Transport and Air Charter to form British United Airways, which continued to operate the 'Blue Nile' service for Sudan Airways.

✧ **BEA Airtours/British Airtours**: BEA Airtours was established as a subsidiary of the state airline BEA in 1969 to compete for a share in the lucrative inclusive-tour charter market. It began operating from its Gatwick base on 5 March 1970 with a fleet of ex-BEA Comet 4B aircraft, but was soon looking for larger aircraft with which to replace the Comets on European routes and also to enable expansion into long-haul charters. From the summer of 1972 a number of ex-BOAC Boeing 707s were acquired for these purposes. When BEA and BOAC merged in 1974 to form British Airways the charter subsidiary was renamed British Airtours.

✧ **British Caledonian Airways Ltd**: Was formed in November 1970 when Caledonian Airways took over British United Airways. The new airline was initially known as Caledonian/BUA but this was soon changed. A fleet of thirty-one jets operated scheduled services within the UK and to Continental Europe, Africa, South America and the USA. Wide-bodied operations began in March 1977 when DC-10s were introduced on to flights to Nigeria and Ghana. Charter flights were also operated, but were dropped in 1978. During 1979 BCAL became the UK launch customer for the Airbus A310. In 1980 services to Dubai and St Louis were inaugurated.

✧ **British Island Airways**: In July 1970 British United Island Airways, the UK regional arm of British United Airways, was renamed British Island Airways. When Caledonian Airways took over British United Airways in November of that year BIA was not included in the takeover and continued operating as a separate company. A fleet of Handley Page Herald aircraft was used on seasonal services to the Channel Islands and the Isle of Man, but the link between Gatwick and Guernsey was operated year-round. BIA also operated a small fleet of Dakota aircraft on freight services, carrying flowers from the Channel Islands into Gatwick and delivering newspapers to British army bases in Germany. In 1979 four BAC One-Eleven jets were acquired for use on inclusive-tour contracts.

✧ **British United Airways**: Was formed on 1 July 1960 by the merger of Airwork and Hunting-Clan Air Transport. Scheduled services were operated from Gatwick to East, Central, and West Africa; Gibraltar; Rotterdam; Le Touquet and the Channel Islands. In April 1965 BUA became the first airline in the world to introduce the BAC One-Eleven 'bus-stop' jet. Long-haul VC-10s were also operated, initially on trooping flights, then on scheduled services to Africa and South America from the spring of 1965. The airline also operated an extensive inclusive-tour charter programme, using specially acquired One-Eleven series 500s from 1968. On 30 November 1970 BUA was taken over by Caledonian Airways (Prestwick). The merged airline was briefly called Caledonian/BUA, but this was soon changed to British Caledonian Airways.

✧ **Caledonian Airways (Prestwick)**: Was established in 1961 as a charter operator, and commenced services in late November of that year with a flight to Barbados. Initially Douglas DC-7Cs leased from the Belgian airline SABENA were used, and during 1962 charters were operated to the Mediterranean resorts and North America, where the airline traded upon its Scottish links to attract ethnic group travel. By the summer of 1965 four DC-7Cs and three turbo-prop Britannias were in service, and in January 1966 the airline acquired its first Boeing 707. In March 1969 BAC One-Eleven series 500s were placed on to Mediterranean inclusive-tour flights. In November 1970 Caledonian took over British United Airways to form Caledonian/BUA, soon to be renamed British Caledonian Airways.

✧ **Ciro's Aviation**: Was formed in December 1946 and was run from its parent Ciro's Club in London. Passenger and freight ad hoc charters from Gatwick commenced in January 1947 using a single Dakota aircraft. During 1950 the airline signed an agreement with Pilot Travel for the operation of inclusive-tour flights to the Italian Dolomites. In January 1951 Ciro's Aviation sold its two Dakotas and ceased operations.

✧ **Dan-Air Services**: Was established in 1953 by ship-brokers Davies and Newman, and took its name from their initials. The airline's first base was at Southend Airport, transferring to Blackbushe Airport in 1955. On the closure of Blackbushe on 31 May 1960 the airline moved again, this time to Gatwick, from where charter flights and a scheduled service to Jersey were operated. An engineering base was set up at nearby Lasham Airfield to service the expanding fleet which grew to include Dakotas, Airspeed Ambassadors, Avro Yorks, and Bristol 170s. Dan-Air moved into the jet age with the acquisition of a large fleet of de Havilland Comets for inclusive-tour operations. By the mid-1970s Dan-Air was Britain's largest charter airline. Boeing 727 and BAC One-Eleven jets later joined the holiday charter fleet, and Boeing 707s were used for a short time on long-haul group charters.

✧ **Donaldson International Airlines**: Was established in 1964, but initially leased out its aircraft to other airlines and did not begin operating under its own name until April 1969. A base was established at Gatwick and a fleet of three Britannia turbo-prop aircraft operated many inclusive-tour flights as well as transatlantic group charters. In May 1971 Boeing 707s entered service and by the end of the year four were in operation and the Britannias were retired. However, on 8 August 1974 Donaldson International ceased operations.

✧ **Eros Airlines (UK)**: Was launched on 2 March 1962 and used Vickers Vikings on inclusive-tour flights out of Gatwick. By that summer three examples were in service. Eros Airlines was the last Gatwick-based Viking operator and had plans to replace them with turbo-prop aircraft, but ceased operations on 4 April 1964.

✧ **Falcon Airways**: Was founded in 1959 and transferred its base to Gatwick on the closure of Blackbushe Airport in 1960. Inclusive-tour charters were operated with a fleet of Viking and Hermes aircraft. In 1961 Lockheed Constellations were acquired, but after operational problems with these the airline's Air Operators Certificate was withdrawn in September 1961 and it went into receivership in January 1962.

✧ **Hornton Airways**: Was formed at Gatwick in late 1946 as an air taxi and air charter operator, and initially used Percival Proctor and Airspeed Consul aircraft. The Consuls were later used on holiday charters to Austria and Switzerland, and a Dakota was also acquired. However, in early 1950 the company's operations began to be run down, and by the end of May all flying had ceased.

✧ **IAS Cargo Airlines**: Began freight charters out of Gatwick to several points in Africa in June 1972, using Britannia turbo-prop aircraft. By the spring of 1973 three Britannias were in service and points in the Middle East were also being served. During 1975 Douglas DC-8 jet freighters were introduced. In 1976 IAS was operating twenty-five services each month to Nigeria, and ten flights to East Africa, using DC-8s, Britannias and Canadair CL-44s. In August 1979 IAS merged with Stansted-based Trans-Meridian Air Cargo to form British Cargo Airlines, but this company went out of business in March 1980.

✧ **Laker Airways**: Was established in February 1966 by Mr Freddie Laker, the former Managing Director of British United Airways. An operating base was set up at Gatwick and the first aircraft acquired were two elderly Bristol Britannias. Operations with these commenced in July 1966, but the airline soon bought One-Eleven jets and with them pioneered the 'time-charter' method of hiring them out to tour operators. One-Eleven services started in March 1967, and by 1976 there were five examples in the fleet. Boeing 707s were also used, and on 21 November 1972 Laker Airways operated Europe's first revenue service by a wide-bodied DC-10 aircraft, a charter to Palma with 331 passengers. In September 1977 the airline's DC-10s were used to inaugurate its Skytrain 'walk-on' service to New York. In 1978 Laker ordered a fleet of Airbus A300s for use on a proposed European Skytrain network. During that year the USA Skytrain services were expanded to serve Los Angeles and Miami, and by October 1980 fully pre-bookable fares were available on all Skytrain routes.

✧ **Lloyd International Airways**: Was founded in January 1961 and was initially based at Cambridge Airport, using Douglas DC-4 aircraft. By 1963 the operating base had been transferred to Gatwick. Britannia turbo-props and Boeing 707 jets were later acquired, but the airline then moved its base to Stansted in 1965 before ceasing operations in June 1972.

✧ **Morton Air Services**: Had a long history, being established at Croydon Airport in May 1945. A fleet of Dragon Rapide, Airspeed Consul, Dove and Heron aircraft was operated from there over the years, and when Croydon closed in September 1959 the base was transferred to Gatwick. From there, scheduled services were operated to Rotterdam, Swansea and the Channel Islands with Doves and Herons. On 1 July 1960 Morton Air Services became part of the British United Airways group, but continued to operate under its own name for the time being. Three Dakotas were acquired in 1962, but on 1 November that year all the aircraft were transferred to British United Airways or sold off, and the Morton Air Services name disappeared.

✧ **Orion Airways**: Commenced holiday charter operations with Vickers Vikings from Blackbushe Airport in August 1957. When Blackbushe Airport closed in May 1960 Orion transferred its operations to Gatwick and continued inclusive-tour flying from there, but ceased operations in November 1960.

✧ **Overseas Aviation**: Was established in 1957 and was initially based at Southend Airport. The company transferred its operations to Gatwick in 1960, and in June of that year it opened a large hangar of Scandinavian design there to house its large fleet of Vickers Vikings and Canadair Argonauts. In July 1961 Overseas inaugurated a 'walk-on' scheduled service between Prestwick and Gatwick, but this was short-lived and the airline ceased operations in August of that year.

✧ **Pegasus Airlines**: Was founded in 1958 and was initially based at Luton Airport. The airline then moved to Blackbushe Airport, and then to Gatwick when Blackbushe closed in May 1960. A fleet of three Vickers Vikings was built up before the airline moved yet again in August 1960, this time to Blackpool Airport, but charter flights were still operated out of Gatwick, and in October 1960 a scheduled service linking Blackpool and Gatwick was inaugurated. This was suspended for the winter but resumed for the summer of 1961, but in October 1961 Pegasus Airlines ceased all operations.

✧ **Scillonian Air Services**: Was set up in June 1962 to provide a scheduled air link between Gatwick and the Isles of Scilly. An Aero Commander 500A executive aircraft was used, initially operating charter flights until the scheduled service began in September 1963. This continued until the autumn of 1964. The service was then run down and the airline ceased operations in December 1964.

✧ **Sky Charters**: Was an air taxi and executive charter company which was formed at Gatwick in July 1962 with one Piper Apache aircraft. In January 1963 Sky Charters took over the operation of several Beech aircraft on behalf of the Light Aircraft Division of Short Brothers and Harland Ltd, who were the UK distributors for all Beech aircraft types. Their demonstration aircraft were transferred to Gatwick and were used for many charter flights from there. However, operations were run down from June 1965 and ceased altogether in August of that year.

✧ **Swiss Universal Air Charters**: Was founded in 1957 with Vickers Viking aircraft and moved to Gatwick from Southend Airport. From the summer of 1960 inclusive-tour flights were operated from Gatwick to Basle, but Swiss Universal ceased trading in September 1961.

✧ **Trader Airways**: Was an executive jet charter operator which was formed at Gatwick in late 1970. A fleet of leased Falcon 20 and HS 125 executive jets and Piper Navajo piston-engined aircraft was built up and many charters were operated from Gatwick until Trader Airways ceased operations in May 1974.

✧ **Tradewinds Airways**: Was established in November 1968 to take over and operate the Canadair CL-44 turbo-props of the defunct Transglobe Airways. By the end of 1970 five of these aircraft were in service on cargo flights from Gatwick to Africa and the Middle and Far East. In 1977 the airline became part of the Lonrho Group and began to replace its CL-44s with Boeing 707 freighters.

Services to Chicago and Toronto were added, and during the 1980s Tradewinds grew to become the UK's largest cargo airline.

✧ **Transcontinental Air Services**: Was a small passenger and freight charter operator which started operations from Gatwick with an Airspeed Consul in early 1947. Operations ceased in the spring of 1949.

✧ **Trans-European Airways**: Was established at Swansea Airport in early 1959 with de Havilland Rapide biplanes. In 1960 the base was transferred to Coventry Airport. Larger aircraft in the form of Bristol 170 and Lockheed Constellation equipment was acquired, and Gatwick was selected as the base for the Constellations. The airline's first Constellation service was operated from Gatwick to Berlin on 17 July 1961. In late July 1962 a Receiver was appointed for the airline. Operations ceased during the following month, and the Bristol 170 and one of the Constellations were impounded at Gatwick.

✧ **Transglobe Airways**: Began life in August 1958 as Air Links. In May 1959 an ex-Aer Lingus Dakota was purchased and used for ad hoc passenger and freight charters out of Gatwick. Expansion came in 1962 with the acquisition of four-engined Handley Page Hermes aircraft, followed by Canadair Argonauts from January 1964. With these aircraft a programme of inclusive-tour charters was operated from Gatwick. For the summer 1965 season turbo-prop Bristol Britannias were purchased, and in August 1965 the company name was changed to Transglobe Airways. In May 1967 an agreement was signed with the US operator Seaboard World Airlines for the lease-purchase of six Canadair CL-44 turbo-prop airliners. In July 1967 Transglobe took over the Gatwick-based Air Couriers aircraft maintenance organisation. By the summer of 1968 three CL-44s were in service on low-fare transatlantic passenger flights, but on 28 November 1968 Transglobe abruptly ceased operations.

✧ **Union Air Services**: Was founded at Gatwick in late 1946 with two D.H. 86B biplane aircraft. Many charters were operated, especially to racecourses throughout Britain. In August 1947 Handley Page Halifax converted bombers were acquired, but in October of that year the airline's fleet was absorbed into that of Bond Air Services.

✧ **World Wide Aviation**: Was founded in July 1960 and commenced charter operations in December of that year. Inclusive-tour flights were operated out of Gatwick with Douglas DC-4s until the airline ceased operations in July 1962.

APPENDIX 2

SQUADRONS AT GATWICK DURING THE SECOND WORLD WAR

No. 2 Squadron: April–July 1944: Mustang I, Mustang II

No. 4 Squadron: April–June 1944: Spitfire XI, Mosquito XVI

No. 14 Squadron: August–October 1945: Mosquito VI

No. 18 Squadron: May–June 1940: Blenheim IV

No. 19 Squadron: October 1943: Spitfire IX

No. 26 Squadron: Various times from September 1940–June 1943: Lysander I, II, III, then Tomahawk I, IIA, then Mustang I

No. 53 Squadron: June–July 1940: Blenheim IV

No. 57 Squadron: May–June 1940: Blenheim IV

No. 63 Squadron: June–July 1942: Mustang I, IA

No. 65 Squadron: October 1943: Spitfire IX

No. 80 Squadron: June–July 1944: Spitfire IX

No. 92 Squadron: Detachment only, January–March 1940: Blenheim I, Spitfire

No. 98 Squadron: June–July 1940: Battle I

No. 116 Squadron: August–September 1944: Oxford

No. 141 Squadron: Several detachments September 1940–November 1940: Defiant I

No. 168 Squadron: March 1944: Mustang I

No. 171 Squadron: June–December 1942: Tomahawk I, IIA, then Mustang IA

No. 175 Squadron: December 1942–January 1943: Hurricane IIB

No. 183 Squadron: April–May 1943: Typhoon IA, IB

No. 229 Squadron: June–July 1944: Spitfire IX

No. 239 Squadron: Various times from January 1941–June 1943: Lysander I, IIA, then Tomahawk I, IIA, then Hurricane I, IIC, then Mustang I

No. 268 Squadron: April–June 1944: Mustang I, IA

No. 274 Squadron: June–July 1944: Spitfire IX

No. 287 Squadron: Detachments only from August 1944–January 1945: Oxford I, II, Martinet I, Tempest V, Beaufighter I, Spitfire IX

No. 309 Squadron: December 1942: Mustang I, IA

No. 400 Squadron RCAF: May 1942–June 1942: Mustang I
No. 414 Squadron RCAF: Various times from May 1943–April 1944: Mustang I
No. 430 Squadron RCAF: Various times from July 1943–April 1944: Mustang I
No. 655 Squadron AOP: March–April 1943: Auster III

Many other support units were based at Gatwick or passed through. These included:

No. 49 Maintenance Unit
No. 404 Aircraft Stores Park
No. 1 Aircraft Delivery Unit
No. 1 Anti-aircraft Calibration Unit
No. 8 Anti-aircraft Calibration Flight
No. 71 Group (Army Co-operation)
Nos. 35 and 36 Army Co-operation Wings
No. 123 Airfield HQ
No. 129 Airfield HQ
British Air Forces of Occupation Communications Squadron/Wing
Civilian Repair Organisation: Airwork General Trading Co. Ltd, and Southern
    Aircraft (Gatwick) Ltd.
No. 19 Elementary and Reserve Flying Training School
No. 162 Gliding School
No. 83 Group Rear HQ
No. 83 Group Communications Flight
No. 84 Group Communications Flight
No. 403 Repair and Salvage Unit
SHAEF Communications Squadron
No. 70 (Bomber) Wing

(Source: Gatwick Aviation Society)

APPENDIX 3

THE HANGARS AT GATWICK 1958–80

Hangar 1 (the Transair Hangar) was already in use at the time of the official opening of the redeveloped airport in June 1958. It was built of pre-stressed concrete and was 280ft long with 110ft-wide clear space. It originally incorporated hydraulic lifts to lower the undercarriage of Viscount aircraft below floor level to enable the engines to be worked on without the need for steps. The main contractor was Sir Alfred McAlpine & Sons Ltd. The total cost was £250,000. It was later used by British United Airways in the 1960s for their BAC One-Eleven fleet, and then by BCAL and British Airways as a motor transport depot. It then fell into disrepair, and dismantling began in 2013.

Hangar 2 was also built for Transair, in 1960, and was 240ft long by 58ft deep. The main contractor was Howard Farrow Ltd of London NW11. Around 1967 the frontage was modified by the removal of the doors and the addition of a 24ft-wide two-storey office block facing the apron. The hangar and offices were demolished in 2007.

Hangar 3 (the BUA VC-10 Hangar) was conceived when British United Airways ordered VC-10 aircraft and realised that their existing facilities would be inadequate to house them, especially the tails. Construction began in 1964 and was completed by June 1965. It was considered to be the largest of its type in the UK, if not Europe. It was a steel-framed building, consisting of three bays, and was 180ft wide. The three bays were designed so that a VC-10 could enter tail-first in the middle bay (fitting between the main central columns) with its wings in the outer bays. The architects were Mr Clive Pascall and Mr Peter Watson and the steel fabricator was Constel (Structures) Ltd. Around 1967 the hangar was doubled in width, to 360ft, with six bays. A pair of tail docks were later fitted on full-length rails, allowing for the enclosure of the tails of longer or taller aircraft. The hangar was demolished in early 2007.

Hangar 4 was built for Overseas Aviation and was constructed of timber. It was opened in June 1960 and was described as the largest timber parallel chord portal frame in Europe. It had a clear span of 150ft and was 150ft long, and was designed to accommodate two Canadair Argonaut aircraft placed diagonally or one Britannia nose on. The main contractor was J. Jarvis & Sons Ltd and the timber fabricators was Beves' at Shoreham. Overseas Aviation was wound up in October 1961 and the hangar was afterwards used by Morton Air Services and others. It was burnt down in the 1980s.

Hangar 5 was situated next door to Hangar 3, and was built in 1980 for British Caledonian. It was intended to house wide-bodied DC-10 aircraft and occupied 5,000m². At the rear of the hangar, and linked to it, was a reinforced concrete office complex. The project cost £5.25 million and the main contractor was James Longley & Co. Ltd of Crawley.

In 1962 Air Couriers moved into their new hangar, which may in fact have been an extended version of a long hangar that was present in 1961. An extension on the south side, at right angles to the main building, was added later. In August 1967 Air Couriers was taken over by Transglobe Airways. Two bays of the hangar were rented to Laker Airways. By May 1968 another extension was under way. The hangar was demolished in 2007.

Laker Hangar, Hangar 6: In August 1968 work started on an 11-acre site for Laker Airways. The first phase was completed by March 1969 and the whole hangar was complete by April 1969. It comprised three bays with six sliding doors and measured 180ft by 204ft with an overall height of 61ft. The architects were Mr Clive Pascall and Mr Peter Watson. In November 1977 a contract to extend the hangar was awarded to Mears. This extension doubled its width and enabled it to accommodate two DC-10s. The hangar was later to be used by British Airways.

The BEA Helicopters/British Airways Helicopters Hangar: BEA Helicopters established a base near to the original 'Beehive' terminal when they moved to Gatwick from Peterborough, and in May 1978 British Airways Helicopters began to redevelop the site with the construction of a new complex. The north part of the old office building and five bays of the existing Bellman hangar were demolished. The rest of the Bellman hangar remained in use with a partition to shut off the end. The new hangar, on the west side within the complex, had dimensions of 44m by 30m and headroom of 9.7m. The hangar was designed to accommodate a Boeing Chinook plus two other helicopters. Phase 1 was opened in April 1979, and Phase 2 in August 1980. During Phase 2 the remainder of the Bellman hangar was demolished. The total cost of the new complex was £2.5 million. The main contractor was Norwest Holst (Southern) Ltd.

APPENDIX 4

FLEET LISTS OF GATWICK-BASED
AIRLINES IN MAY 1973

BEA Airtours
Comet 4B: G-APMC; G-ARCP; G-ARGM; G-ARJK; G-ARJL. Boeing 707:
G-APFD; G-APFG; G-APFH; G-APFK; G-APFL; G-APFO; G-ARWD.

British Caledonian Airways
VC-10: G-ARTA 'Loch Ness' (damaged and out of service); G-ASIW 'Loch
Lomond'; G-ASIX 'Loch Maree'. Boeing 707: G-ATZC 'County of Stirling';
G-AWTK 'Flagship Bonny Scotland'; G-AWWD 'County of Angus'; G-AXRS
'County of Caithness'; G-AYEX 'County of Argyll'; G-AYSI 'County of
Sutherland'; G-AYZZ 'County of Renfrew'; G-AZJM 'County of Ayr'; G-AZRO
'County of Lanark'; G-BAWP 'County of Inverness'. BAC One-Eleven: G-ASJC
'City of Glasgow'; G-ASJE 'City of Dundee'; G-ASJF 'Burgh of Fort William';
G-ASJG 'Burgh of Paisley'; G-ASJH 'Burgh of Hawick'; G-ASJI 'Royal Burgh
of Nairn'; G-ASTJ 'Royal Burgh of Dumfermline'; G-AWWX 'Flagship Isle
of Skye'; G-AWWY 'Isle of Iona'; G-AWWZ 'Isle of Eriskay'; G-AWYR 'Isle
of Tiree'; G-AWYS 'Isle of Bute'; G-AWYT 'Isle of Barra'; G-AWYU 'Isle of
Colonsay'; G-AWYV 'Isle of Harris'; G-AXJK 'Isle of Staffa'; G-AXJL 'Isle of
Mingulay'; G-AXJM 'Isle of Islay'; G-AXYD 'Isle of Arran'; G-AYOP 'Isle of
Hoy'; G-AZMF 'Isle of Raasay'.

Dan-Air Services
Boeing 707: G-AYSL; G-AZTG. Boeing 727: G-BAEF; G-BAFZ; G-BAJW
Comet 4/4B/4C: G-APDB; G-APDG; G-APDK; G-APDM; G-APDO;
G-APMB; G-APMD; G-APME; G-APMF; G-APMG; G-APYC; G-APYD;
G-APZM; G-ARJN; G-AROV; G-AYVS; G-AYWX; G-AZIY; (n.b. some
examples withdrawn from use, some expected to enter service as others are
withdrawn, some purchased for spares use only.) BAC One-Eleven: G-ATPJ;
G-ATPL; G-AXCK; G-AXCP; G-AZED. HS 748: G-ARAY; G-ARMW;
G-ARMX; G-ARRW; G-ASPL; G-AXVG; G-AZSU.

Donaldson International Airways
Boeing 707-321: G-AYVG 'Carillon II'; G-AZWA 'Nike II'.

International Aviation Services
Bristol Britannia: G-AOVF; G-AOVP; G-AOVS; G-ATMA.

Laker Airways
McDonnell-Douglas DC-10-10: G-AZZC 'Eastern Belle'; G-AZZD 'Western Belle'. Boeing 707-138B: G-AVZZ; G-AWDG. BAC One-Eleven: G-ATPK; G-AVBW; G-AVBX; G-AVBY; G-AVYZ.

Tradewinds Airways
Canadair CL-44D-4: G-AWDK; G-AWDS; G-AWGT; G-AWOV; G-AWSC.

Total number of each type based at Gatwick:
DC-10: two
BAC One-Eleven: thirty-one
Bristol Britannia: four
Boeing 707: twenty three
Boeing 727: three
Canadair CL-44: five
DH Comet: nineteen
HS 748: seven
VC-10: two
Total: ninety-six

APPENDIX 5

AIR TRANSPORT MOVEMENTS AT GATWICK IN AUGUST 1963

(excluding Gatwick-based airlines and light/executive aircraft, but including military transport types)

At this time, the movements into the airport were almost exclusively operated by propeller-driven airliners.

✧ **Thur 1 Aug**: 10911 Douglas Dakota, Royal Canadian Air Force. HB-AAG Handley Page Herald, Globe Air. LX-SAF Douglas DC-4, Luxair. N6917C Lockheed Super Constellation, Flying Tiger Line. OY-AOE Douglas DC-6, Nordair. SE-BDH Douglas DC-6, Transair Sweden.

✧ **Fri 2 Aug**: 10291 Dakota, Royal Canadian Air Force. 55-3307 de Havilland Canada Otter, US Army. EC-ACF Douglas DC-4, Aviaco. EC-ASS Douglas DC-6, Aviaco. EC-ATR Douglas DC-7C, Spantax. F-BGSN Douglas DC-6, Air Afrique. F-BGTY Douglas DC-6, UAT. F-BHEE Douglas DC-6, TAI. F-BKBQ Douglas DC-6, Airnautic. G-AMLJ Bristol 170, BKS Air Transport. HB-ILB Douglas DC-4, Balair. I-DIMD/E/P/U Douglas DC-6Bs, SAM. OY-AFB Canadair Argonaut, Flying Enterprise. OY-AOE Douglas DC-6, Nordair.

✧ **Sat 3 Aug**: CF-PCI Douglas DC-6, Wardair. D-ANIP Vickers Viscount, Condor. EC-ACD Douglas DC-4, Aviaco. EC-AIO Lockheed Super Constellation, Iberia. EC-ASS Douglas DC-6, Aviaco. EC-AUC Douglas DC-6, TASSA. F-BGSN Douglas DC-6, Air Afrique. F-BHEE/F Douglas DC-6s, TAI. F-BIPT/BJES Vickers Vikings, Airnautic. F-BKBQ Douglas DC-6, Airnautic. G-ALYF Dakota, British Westpoint Airlines. G-AMLJ Bristol 170, BKS Air Transport. G-AMWH Bristol 171 helicopter, BEA. G-ANVR Bristol 170 Superfreighter, British United Air Ferries. G-ARIR Vickers Viscount, Starways. HB-IBZ Douglas DC-6B, Balair. HB-IEM Airspeed Ambassador, Globe Air. HB-ILB/U Douglas DC-4s, Balair. I-DIMA/D/E/I/U Douglas DC-6Bs, SAM. SE-BDO Douglas DC-6, Transair Sweden. VP-YTY Douglas DC-4, Rhodesian Air Services. YU-AFE Douglas DC-6B, Adria Airways.

✧ **Sun 4 Aug**: EC-ACD Douglas DC-4, Aviaco. EC-ASS Douglas DC-6, Aviaco. EC-ATR Douglas DC-7C, Spantax. EC-AUC Douglas DC-6, TASSA. F-BGSN Douglas DC-6, Air Afrique. F-BHEE/F Douglas DC-6s, TAI. F-BIPT/BJES Vickers Vikings, Airnautic. F-BKBQ Douglas DC-6, Airnautic. HB-IBZ Douglas DC-6B, Balair. HB-ILU Douglas DC-4, Balair. I-DIMA/D/E/I/U Douglas DC-6Bs, SAM. I-TIVA Handley Page Herald, Itavia. N6916C Lockheed Super Constellation, Flying Tiger Line. VP-MAA Douglas DC-4, Malta Metropolitan Airways. YU-AFF Douglas DC-6B, Adria Airways.

✧ **Mon 5 Aug**: 10911 Dakota, Royal Canadian Air Force. CF-PCI Douglas DC-6, Wardair. EC-AIO Lockheed Super Constellation, Iberia. EC-AVA Douglas DC-6, TASSA. F-BGSN Douglas DC-6, Air Afrique. F-BHEF Douglas DC-6, TAI. G-ALYF Dakota, British Westpoint Airlines. HB-AAG Handley Page Herald, Globe Air. HB-IEL Airspeed Ambassador, Globe Air. I-DIMA/I Douglas DC-6Bs, SAM. VP-MAA Douglas DC-4, Malta Metropolitan Airways.

✧ **Tue 6 Aug**: 17506 Canadair North Star, Royal Canadian Air Force. G-AJHY Dakota, British Westpoint Airlines. HB-AAH Handley Page Herald, Globe Air. I-DIME Douglas DC-6B, SAM. LN-SUI Douglas DC-6, Braathens SAFE. OY-AOF Douglas DC-6, Nordair. SE-BDH Douglas DC-6, Transair Sweden.

✧ **Wed 7 Aug**: 17515 Canadair North Star, Royal Canadian Air Force. 662 Dakota, Royal Canadian Air Force. F-BIPT/BJRS Vickers Vikings, Airnautic. G-AMSA Bristol 170, British United Air Ferries. HB-IEK Airspeed Ambassador, Globe Air. I-DIME Douglas DC-6B, SAM. OY-AOB/F Douglas DC-6s, Nordair. SE-BDI Douglas DC-6, Transair Sweden.

✧ **Thur 8 Aug**: 10302 Lockheed C-130 Hercules, Royal Canadian Air Force. EC-ASS Douglas DC-6, Aviaco. F-BIPT Vickers Viking, Airnautic. HP-379 C-74 Globemaster 1, Aeronaves del Panama. I-TIVA Handley Page Herald, Itavia. LX-SAF Douglas DC-4, Luxair. OY-AOF Douglas DC-6, Nordair. PH-MAA/E Dakotas, Martins Air Charter. VP-YNC Vickers Viscount, Central African Airways.

✧ **Fri 9 Aug**: 662 Dakota, Royal Canadian Air Force. 9850 Bristol 170, Royal Canadian Air Force. CF-PCI Douglas DC-6, Wardair. EC-AEK Douglas DC-4, Aviaco. EC-ATR Douglas DC-7C, Spantax. F-BHEE/F Douglas DC-6s, TAI. F-BHMR Douglas DC-6, Air Afrique. F-BKBQ Douglas DC-6, Airnautic. HB-ILB Douglas DC-4, Balair. I-DIMA/E/P Douglas DC-6Bs, SAM. N6919C Lockheed Super Constellation, Flying Tiger Line. OY-AOF Douglas DC-6, Nordair. OY-KND Douglas DC-7C, SAS.

✧ **Sat 10 Aug**: D-ANUN Vickers Viscount, Condor. EC-AMQ/AQN Lockheed Super Constellations, Iberia. EC-APQ Douglas DC-4, Aviaco. EC-ASS Douglas DC-6, Aviaco. EC-ATR Douglas DC-7C, Spantax. EC-AUC Douglas DC-6, TASSA. F-BHEE/F Douglas DC-6s, TAI. F-BHMR Douglas DC-6, Air Afrique. F-BIPT/BJRS Vickers Vikings, Airnautic. F-BKBQ Douglas DC-6,

Airnautic. G-APZB Vickers Viscount, Starways (diversion from Manchester). HB-IBZ Douglas DC-6B, Balair. HB-ILB/U Douglas DC-4s, Balair. I-DIMA/D/P/U Douglas DC-6Bs, SAM. I-TIVA Handley Page Herald, Itavia. LX-HEP Douglas DC-4, Interocean Airways. N6918C Lockheed Super Constellation, Flying Tiger Line. N90773 Douglas DC-7C, Saturn Airways. SE-BDZ Douglas DC-6, Transair Sweden. YU-AFF Douglas DC-6B, Adria Airways.

❖ **Sun 11 Aug**: CF-PCI Douglas DC-6, Wardair. EC-AEP Douglas DC-4, Aviaco. EC-ASS Douglas DC-6, Aviaco. EC-AUC Douglas DC-6, TASSA. F-BHEE/F Douglas DC-6s, TAI. F-BHMR Douglas DC-6, Air Afrique. HB-AAH Handley Page Herald, Globe Air. HB-IBZ Douglas DC-6B, Balair. HB-ILU Douglas DC-4, Balair. I-DIMA/D/I/P/U Douglas DC-6Bs, SAM. I-TIVA/E Handley Page Heralds, Itavia. LZ-BEK Ilyushin IL-18, TABSO. YU-AFC Douglas DC-6B, Adria Airways.

❖ **Mon 12 Aug**: KN665 Dakota, Royal Canadian Air Force. EC-AMQ Lockheed Super Constellation, Iberia. EC-ATR Douglas DC-7C, Spantax. F-BHEF Douglas DC-6, TAI. F-BHMR Douglas DC-6, Air Afrique. G-ALYF Dakota, British Westpoint Airlines. HB-IBU Douglas DC-6B, Balair. I-DIMA Douglas DC-6B, SAM. TC-YOL Dakota, THY Turkish Airlines.

❖ **Tue 13 Aug**: 15932 Canadair CC-106 Yukon, Royal Canadian Air Force. CF-PCI Douglas DC-6, Wardair. G-ALYF Dakota, British Westpoint Airlines. G-ASIO Aero Commander 500A, Scillonian Air Services. I-DIMU Douglas DC-6B, SAM. LN-SUB Douglas DC-6, Braathens SAFE. OY-AFB Canadair Argonaut, Flying Enterprise. OY-AOC Douglas DC-6, Nordair.

❖ **Wed 14 Aug**: 972 Dakota, Royal Canadian Air Force. 9699 Bristol 170, Royal Canadian Air Force. F-BIPT/BJRS Vickers Vikings, Airnautic. HB-IEK Airspeed Ambassador, Globe Air. I-DIMU Douglas DC-6B, SAM. N5401V Lockheed Super Constellation, Capitol Airways. OY-AFB Canadair Argonaut, Flying Enterprise. OY-AOC Douglas DC-6, Nordair. SE-BDZ Douglas DC-6, Transair Sweden. XP810 de Havilland Canada Beaver, Army Air Corps.

❖ **Thur 15 Aug**: CF-PCI Douglas DC-6, Wardair. EC-ASS Douglas DC-6, Aviaco. F-BJRS Vickers Viking, Airnautic. HB-AAG Handley Page Herald, Globe Air. HB-IEM Airspeed Ambassador, Globe Air. I-DIMU Douglas DC-6B. SAM. LX-SAF Douglas DC-4, Luxair. OY-AOC Douglas DC-6, Nordair. XP810 de Havilland Canada Beaver, Army Air Corps.

❖ **Fri 16 Aug**: XK697 de Havilland Comet C2, RAF. 44-76657 Dakota, USAF. 9698 Bristol 170, Royal Canadian Air Force. 972 Dakota, Royal Canadian Air Force. EC-APQ Douglas DC-4, Aviaco. EC-ATR Douglas DC-7C, Spantax. F-BGSN Douglas DC-6, Air Afrique. F-BHEE/F Douglas DC-6s, TAI. F-BKBQ Douglas DC-6, Airnautic. G-AMLJ Bristol 170, BKS Air Transport. G-ASIO Aero Commander 500A, Scillonian Air Services. HB-IEM Airspeed Ambassador, Globe Air. HB-ILU Douglas DC-4, Balair. I-DIMA/D/E/U

Douglas DC-6Bs, SAM. OY-AOC Douglas DC-6, Nordair. SE-BDI Douglas DC-6, Transair Sweden.

✧ **Sat 17 Aug**: EC-AEP Douglas DC-4, Aviaco. EC-AMQ Lockheed Super Constellation, Iberia. EC-ASS Douglas DC-6, Aviaco. EC-AVA Douglas DC-6, TASSA. F-BGSN Douglas DC-6, Air Afrique. F-BHEE/F Douglas DC-6s, TAI. F-BIPT/BJRS Vickers Vikings, Airnautic. F-BKBQ Douglas DC-6, Airnautic. G-ALYF Dakota, British Westpoint Airlines. HB-IBU Douglas DC-6B, Balair. HB-ILU/U Douglas DC-4s, Balair. I-DIMD/E/I/U Douglas DC-6Bs, SAM. N318A Douglas DC-7, Overseas National Airways. SE-BDM Douglas DC-6, Transair Sweden.

✧ **Sun 18 Aug**: EC-ACE Douglas DC-4, Aviaco. EC-AMQ Lockheed Super Constellation, Iberia. EC-ASS Douglas DC-6, Aviaco. EC-ATR Douglas DC-7C, Spantax. EC-AVA Douglas DC-6, TASSA. F-BGSN Douglas DC-6, Air Afrique. F-BHEE/F Douglas DC-6s, TAI. F-BIPT/BJRS Vickers Vikings, Airnautic. F-BKBQ Douglas DC-6, Airnautic. HB-IBU Douglas DC-6B, Balair. HB-ILB Douglas DC-4, Balair. I-DIMD/E/I/P/U Douglas DC-6Bs, SAM. I-TIVE Handley Page Herald, Itavia. N315A Douglas DC-7, Overseas National Airways. N5402V Lockheed Super Constellation, Capitol Airways. YU-AFC/D Douglas DC-6Bs, Adria Airways.

✧ **Mon 19 Aug**: 972/KG634 Dakotas, Royal Canadian Air Force. EC-AMQ Lockheed Super Constellation, Iberia. EC-AVA Douglas DC-6, TASSA. F-BGSN Douglas DC-6, Air Afrique. F-BHEE Douglas DC-6, TAI. I-DIMU Douglas DC-6B, SAM. SE-CCY/Z Douglas DC-6s, Transair Sweden.

✧ **Tue 20 Aug**: G-AJHY Dakota, British Westpoint Airlines. I-DIMU Douglas DC-6B, SAM. LN-SUB Douglas DC-6, Braathens SAFE. OH-LRG Convair 440, Finnair. OY-AOF Douglas DC-6, Nordair.

✧ **Wed 21 Aug**: 662 Dakota, Royal Canadian Air Force. 9699 Bristol 170, Royal Canadian Air Force. F-BIPT/BJES Vickers Vikings, Airnautic. G-ASIO Aero Commander 500A, Scillonian Air Services. I-DIMU Douglas DC-6B, SAM. N4903C Lockheed Super Constellation, Capitol Airways. OY-AOB Douglas DC-6, Nordair.

✧ **Thur 22 Aug**: 15932 Canadair CC-106 Yukon, Royal Canadian Air Force. 972 Dakota, Royal Canadian Air Force. CF-PCI Douglas DC-6, Wardair. EC-ASS Douglas DC-6, Aviaco. F-BIPT Vickers Viking, Airnautic. G-AMSA Bristol 170, British United Air Ferries. HB-IEK Airspeed Ambassador, Globe Air. LX-SAF Douglas DC-4, Luxair. OH-LEB Caravelle, Finnair. OY-AOF Douglas DC-6, Nordair. OY-KNC Douglas DC-7C, SAS.

✧ **Fri 23 Aug**: 662 Dakota, Royal Canadian Air Force. 9700 Bristol 170, Royal Canadian Air Force. EC-ACD Douglas DC-4, Aviaco. EC-ATR Douglas DC-7C, Spantax. F-BGSL/N Douglas DC-6s, Air Afrique. F-BHEF Douglas DC-6, TAI. F-BKJZ Douglas DC-6, Airnautic. G-ANVR Bristol 170 Superfreighter, British

United Air Ferries. G-ASIO Aero Commander 500A, Scillonian Air Services. HB-ILU Douglas DC-4, Balair. I-DIME/I/P/U Douglas DC-6Bs, SAM. OY-AOF Douglas DC-6, Nordair.

✧ **Sat 24 Aug**: 10911 Dakota, Royal Canadian Air Force. D-ANUR Vickers Viscount, Condor. EC-AEK Douglas DC-4, Aviaco. EC-ARN Lockheed Super Constellation, Iberia. EC-ASS Douglas DC-6, Aviaco. EC-AVA Douglas DC-6, TASSA. F-BGSL/N Douglas DC-6s, Air Afrique. F-BHEF Douglas DC-6, TAI. F-BIPT/BJES Vickers Vikings, Airnautic. F-BKJZ Douglas DC-6, Airnautic. HB-IBU Douglas DC-6B, Balair. HB-ILB/U Douglas DC-4s, Balair. I-DIMA/D/P/T/U Douglas DC-6Bs, SAM. YU-AFF Douglas DC-6B, Adria Airways.

✧ **Sun 25 Aug**: EC-AEP Douglas DC-4, Aviaco. EC-AMP Lockheed Super Constellation, Iberia. EC-ASS Douglas DC-6, Aviaco. EC-ATR Douglas DC-7C, Spantax. EC-AVA Douglas DC-6, TASSA. F-BGSL Douglas DC-6, Air Afrique. F-BGSN/BHEF Douglas DC-6s, TAI. F-BIPT/BJES Vickers Vikings, Airnautic. F-BJKZ Douglas DC-6, Airnautic. HB-AAG Handley Page Herald, Globe Air. HB-IBU Douglas DC-6B, Balair. HB-ILB Douglas DC-4, Balair. I-DIMA/D/E/P/U Douglas DC-6Bs, SAM. I-TIVA Handley Page Herald, Itavia. LZ-BEM Ilyushin IL-18, Tabso. N90774 Douglas DC-7, Saturn Airways. YU-AFC/E Douglas DC-6Bs, Adria Airways.

✧ **Mon 26 Aug**: 972 Dakota, Royal Canadian Air Force. EC-AMP Lockheed Super Constellation, Iberia. F-BGSL/N Douglas DC-6s, Air Afrique. I-DIMU Douglas DC-6B, SAM. N9718C Lockheed Super Constellation, Capitol Airways. OE-IFA Lockheed Constellation, Austrian Aero Transport.

✧ **Tue 27 Aug**: CF-PCI Douglas DC-6, Wardair. G-ANVR Bristol 170 Superfreighter, British United Air Ferries. I-DIMU Douglas DC-6B, SAM. LN-SUB Douglas DC-6, Braathens SAFE. OH-LEC Caravelle, Finnair. OY-AFB Canadair Argonaut, Flying Enterprise. OY-AOF Douglas DC-6, Nordair. XR136 Armstrong Whitworth Argosy, RAF.

✧ **Wed 28 Aug**: 9700 Bristol 170, Royal Canadian Air Force. 972 Dakota, Royal Canadian Air Force. F-BJER/S Vickers Vikings, Airnautic. G-ASIO Aero Commander 500A, Scillonian Air Services. HB-AAG Handley Page Herald, Globe Air. I-DIMU Douglas DC-6B, SAM. OH-LEB Caravelle, Finnair. OY-AOF Douglas DC-6, Nordair.

✧ **Thur 29 Aug**: 9699 Bristol 170, Royal Canadian Air Force. EC-ASS Douglas DC-6, Aviaco. F-BJER Vickers Viking, Airnautic. G-ANVR Bristol 170 Superfreighter, British United Air Ferries. G-ARVF Vickers VC-10, BOAC (ILS approaches). G-ASIO Aero Commander 500A, Scillonian Air Services. LX-SAF Douglas DC-4, Luxair. N6918C/N6919C Lockheed Super Constellations, Flying Tiger Line. OY-AOF Douglas DC-6, Nordair. WD480 Handley Page Hastings, RAF.

✧ **Fri 30 Aug**: 9699 Bristol 170, Royal Canadian Air Force. 972 Dakota, Royal Canadian Air Force. EC-ACD Douglas DC-4, Aviaco. EC-ATR Douglas DC-7C, Spantax. F-BGSL/N Douglas DC-6s, Air Afrique. F-BHEE Douglas DC-6, TAI. F-BJKZ Douglas DC-6, Airnautic. HB-AAG Handley Page Herald, Globe Air. HB-IBU Douglas DC-6B, Balair. I-DIMA/E/I/P Douglas DC-6Bs, SAM. OH-LEB Caravelle, Finnair. OY-AOB Douglas DC-6, Nordair.

✧ **Sat 31 Aug**: 51-2574 de Havilland Canada U-6A Beaver, US Army. 55-3303 de Havilland Canada U-1A Otter, US Army. CF-PCI Douglas DC-6, Wardair. D-ANUR Vickers Viscount, Condor. EC-AEO Douglas DC-4, Aviaco. EC-AMP/Q Lockheed Super Constellations, Iberia. EC-ASS Douglas DC-6, Aviaco. EC-AVA Douglas DC-6, TASSA. F-BGSL/N Douglas DC-6s, Air Afrique. F-BHEE Douglas DC-6, TAI. F-BJER/S Vickers Vikings, Airnautic. F-BJKZ Douglas DC-6, Airnautic. G-ALYF Dakota, British Westpoint Airlines. G-ASIO Aero Commander 500A, Scillonian Air Services. HB-IBU/Z Douglas DC-6Bs, Balair. I-DIMD/E/P/U Douglas DC-6Bs, SAM. N1005C Lockheed Super Constellation, Intercontinental. N6918C Lockheed Super Constellation, Flying Tiger Line. N90774 Douglas DC-7, Saturn Airways. SE-CFA Curtis C-46 Commando, United Nations.

APPENDIX 6

AIR TRANSPORT MOVEMENTS AT GATWICK IN JULY 1966

(excluding Gatwick-based airlines and light/executive aircraft, but including military transport types)

Three years on from Appendix 5, and airliners such as Caravelles and Boeing 707s are now frequent visitors, but propeller types are still to be seen at the airport.

✧ **Fri 1 Jul**: 4X-ATC Boeing 707, El Al Israel Airlines. 661 Dakota, Royal Canadian Air Force. CF-NAL Lockheed Super Constellation, Nordair. EC-ATV/AVZ Caravelles, Iberia. EC-BCH Douglas DC-7, Trans-Europa. G-AOFW Aviation Traders Carvair, British United Air Ferries. HB-AAL Handley Page Herald, Globe Air. HB-IBZ Douglas DC-6B, Balair. HB-ICX Caravelle, Swissair. HB-ITB Bristol Britannia, Globe Air. I-DIMB Douglas DC-6B, SAM. LX-LGA Fokker F-27, Luxair. N2310B Douglas DC-8, Overseas National Airways. N374WA Boeing 707, World Airways. N804SW Douglas DC-8, Seaboard World Airways. OE-IAM Vickers Viscount, Austrian Airlines. OY-BAV Douglas DC-6, Sterling Airways. OY-KRD/SE-DAC Caravelles, SAS. SE-CNH Douglas DC-7, Osterman Air Charter. WB535 de Havilland Devon, RAF.

✧ **Sat 2 Jul**: 10318 Lockheed C-130 Hercules, Royal Canadian Air Force. KN629 Dakota, Royal Canadian Air Force. 5A-DAA Caravelle, Kingdom of Libya Airlines. 9698 Bristol 170, Royal Canadian Air Force. EC-ATX Caravelle, Iberia. EC-BCH Douglas DC-7, Trans-Europa. EC-BDM Douglas DC-7C, Spantax. G-AOFW Aviation Traders Carvair, British United Air Ferries. G-APED Vickers Vanguard, BEA. HB-AAU Fokker F-27, Balair. HB-IBZ Douglas DC-6B, Balair. HB-ICS Caravelle, Swissair. I-DIMA/B/D/U Douglas DC-6Bs, SAM. LX-LGA Fokker F-27, Luxair. N376WA Boeing 707, World Airways. N8008D Douglas DC-8, Trans International Airways. OH-KDB Douglas DC-6, Kar-Air. OH-LRF Convair 440, Finnair. OY-KRA/SE-DAI Caravelles, SAS. YR-IMA Ilyushin Il-18, Tarom. YU-AFC/E/F Douglas DC-6Bs, Adria Airways.

✧ **Sun 3 Jul**: 15925 Canadair CC-106 Yukon, Royal Canadian Air Force. 7T-VAL Caravelle, Air Algerie. CCCP-42459 Tupolev TU-104, Aeroflot.

CF-CPJ Douglas DC-8, Canadian Pacific Air Lines. CF-FUN Boeing 727, Wardair. CF-PCI Douglas DC-6, Pacific Western Airlines. EC-ARK/ATV/ AXU/AYD/AYE Caravelles, Iberia. G-ALAL Lockheed Constellation, ACE Freighters. G-AOFW Aviation Traders Carvair, British United Air Ferries. G-AOUV Bristol 170 Superfreighter, British United Air Ferries. G-APEA Vickers Vanguard, BEA. HB-IBZ Douglas DC-6B, Balair. I-DIMA/B/U Douglas DC-6Bs, SAM. LN-KLI/R Caravelles, SAS. LX-LGB Fokker F-27, Luxair. LZ-BES Ilyushin IL-18, TABSO. N376WA Boeing 707, World Airways. N4905C Douglas DC-8, Capitol International. OD-AEY Douglas DC-6, Trans Mediterranean Airways. TS-MAC/TAR Caravelles, Tunis Air. YU-AFC/D Douglas DC-6Bs, Adria Airways.

✧ **Mon 4 Jul**: 662/KN269 Dakotas, Royal Canadian Air Force. CF-CPI Douglas DC-8, Canadian Pacific Air Lines. CF-FUN Boeing 727, Wardair. EC-ARJ/ATV Caravelles, Iberia. G-ALAL Lockheed Constellation, ACE Freighters. G-AOFW Aviation Traders Carvair, British United Air Ferries. HA-MOH Ilyushin IL-18, Malev. HB-IBZ Douglas DC-6B, Balair. HB-ICY Caravelle, Swissair. I-DIMU Douglas DC-6B, SAM. N17324 Boeing 707, Continental Airlines. N374WA/ N376WA Boeing 707s, World Airways. N4905C Douglas DC-8, Capitol International. N5035 BAC One-Eleven, American Airlines. N90778 Douglas DC-7, Saturn Airways. OH-LRE Convair 440, Finnair. OH-LSB/F Caravelles, Finnair. OY-BAU Douglas DC-6B, Sterling Airways. OY-KRA/F Caravelles, SAS. PH-DSF Douglas DC-7C, KLM. SE-ERE Douglas DC-7, Transair Sweden. SE-ERN Douglas DC-6, Transair Sweden.

✧ **Tue 5 Jul**: 085 Beech 18, French Air Force. 661/2/KN269 Dakotas, Royal Canadian Air Force. 9698 Bristol 170, Royal Canadian Air Force. CF-FUN Boeing 727, Wardair. EC-AYE Caravelle, Iberia. CF-TAY Douglas DC-7, Transair. EI-APB Dakota, Hibernian Airlines. G-AOFW Aviation Traders Carvair, British United Air Ferries. HA-MOA/H Ilyushin IL-18s, Malev. HB-ICZ Caravelle, Swissair. LN-KLH Caravelle, SAS. N374WA Boeing 707, World Airways. N90803 Douglas DC-7, Saturn Airways. OH-LSE Caravelle, Finnair. SE-CNE Douglas DC-7, Osterman Air Charter.

✧ **Wed 6 Jul**: 662/KN269 Dakotas, Royal Canadian Air Force. 9698 Bristol 170, Royal Canadian Air Force. CF-CPG Douglas DC-8, Canadian Pacific Air Lines. CF-FUN Boeing 727, Wardair. EC-AYE Caravelle, Iberia. G-AOFW Aviation Traders Carvair, British United Air Ferries. HA-MOA/C Ilyushin IL-18s, Malev. HB-ICS/X Caravelles, Swissair. HB-ITB Bristol Britannia, Globe Air. I-DIME Douglas DC-6B, SAM. LN-SUB/K Douglas DC-6s, Braathens SAFE. OE-LAL Vickers Viscount, Austrian Airlines. OY-AND Douglas DC-7, Internord. OY-BAU Douglas DC-6B, Sterling Airways. SE-CNF/H Douglas DC-7s, Osterman Air Charter. SE-DAG Caravelle, SAS.

✧ **Thur 7 Jul**: 5A-DAB Caravelle, Kingdom of Libya Airlines. 661 Dakota, Royal Canadian Air Force. 9698 Bristol 170, Royal Canadian Air Force. F-BASV Breguet Deux Ponts, Air France. G-AHGC de Havilland Rapide, Scillonia Airways. G-AOUV Bristol 170 Superfreighter, British United Air Ferries. HA-MOE Ilyushin IL-18, Malev. HB-AAK Handley Page Herald, Globe Air. HB-IBK Douglas DC-6B, Balair. HB-ICY/Z Caravelles, Swissair. LX-LGY Lockheed Starliner, Luxair. N5034 BAC One-Eleven, American Airlines. N8008D Douglas DC-8, Trans International Airlines. OE-LAL Vickers Viscount, Austrian Airlines. OH-KDC Douglas DC-6, Kar-Air. PH-DSL Douglas DC-7C, Martins Air Charter. SE-CNH Douglas DC-7, Ostermans Air Charter. SE-DAG Caravelle, SAS.

✧ **Fri 8 Jul**: 085 Beech 18, French Air Force. KG441 Dakota, Royal Canadian Air Force. CF-TAY Douglas DC-7, Transair. D-ABAH Douglas DC-6, Sudwestflug. EC-ARK/ATV/AVZ Caravelles, Iberia. EC-BCH Douglas DC-7, Trans Europa. F-BKBI Bristol 170 Superfreighter, Cie Air Transport. G-ALAL Lockheed Constellation, ACE Freighters. G-ARSD Aviation Traders Carvair, British United Air Ferries. HB-AAK Handley Page Herald, Globe Air. HB-IBZ Douglas DC-6B, Balair. HB-ICW Caravelle, Swissair. I-DIME/I Douglas DC-6Bs, SAM. LN-KLI/SE-DAC Caravelles, SAS. LN-SUM Douglas DC-6, Braathens SAFE. LX-LGA Fokker F-27, Luxair. N375WA Boeing 707, World Airways. N90773 Douglas DC-7, Saturn Airways. OY-BAU Douglas DC-6B, Sterling Airways. SE-CNG/H Douglas DC-7s, Osterman Air Charter. SE-ERK/M Douglas DC-7s, Transair Sweden.

✧ **Sat 9 Jul**: 10314 Lockheed C-130 Hercules, Royal Canadian Air Force. 662/KN269 Dakotas, Royal Canadian Air Force. 9698/9850 Bristol 170s, Royal Canadian Air Force. 5A-DAB Caravelle, Kingdom of Libya Airlines. CF-CPG Douglas DC-8. Canadian Pacific Air Lines. CF-FUN Boeing 727, Wardair. CF-PWM Douglas DC-7, Pacific Western Airlines. EC-ATQ Douglas DC-7C, Spantax. EC-ATX Caravelle, Iberia. G-ALAL Lockheed Constellation, ACE Freighters. G-AOUV Bristol 170 Superfreighter, British United Air Ferries. G-APEC Vickers Vanguard, BEA. G-ARSD Aviation Traders Carvair, British United Air Ferries. HB-AAU Fokker F-27, Balair. HB-IBZ Douglas DC-6B, Balair. HB-ICX Caravelle, Swissair. I-DIMB/D/E/I/U Douglas DC-6Bs, SAM. LX-LGA Fokker F-27, Luxair. N373WA Boeing 707, World Airways. OH-KDC Douglas DC-6, Kar-Air. OY-KRG/SE-DAF Caravelles, SAS. YR-IME Ilyushin IL-18, Tarom. YU-AFC/D/E Douglas DC-6s, Adria Airways.

✧ **Sun 10 Jul**: 15924 Canadair CC-106 Yukon, Royal Canadian Air Force. 7T-VAK/L Caravelles, Air Algerie. CF-CPF Douglas DC-8, Canadian Pacific Air Lines. EC-ARJ/ARK/ATX/AVZ Caravelles, Iberia. G-ALAL Lockheed Constellation, ACE Freighters. G-APEJ Vickers Vanguard, BEA. G-ARSD Aviation Traders Carvair, British United Air Ferries. HB-AAU Fokker F-27, Balair.

HB-IBZ Douglas DC-6B, Balair. HB-ICX/Y Caravelles, Swissair. I-DIMA/B/ E/I Douglas DC-6Bs, SAM. LZ-BEP Ilyushin IL-18, Tabso. N374WA Boeing 707, World Airways. N8008D Douglas DC-8, Trans International Airlines. OY-KRD/G Caravelles, SAS. YU-AFC/F Douglas DC-6s, Adria Airways.

✧ **Mon 11 Jul**: 662 Dakota, Royal Canadian Air Force. 7T-VAK Caravelle, Air Algerie. CF-CPF Douglas DC-8, Canadian Pacific Air Lines. CF-FUN Boeing 727, Wardair. EC-ARI/ATX Caravelles, Iberia. F-BHRR/BJTS Caravelles, Air France. HA-MOC Ilyushin IL-18, Malev. HB-IBZ Douglas DC-6B, Balair. HB-ICX Caravelle, Swissair. I-DIMD/E Douglas DC-6Bs, SAM. N17324 Boeing 707, Continental Airlines. N8008D Douglas DC-8, Trans International Airlines. N802SW Douglas DC-8, Seaboard World Airways. OD-AES Douglas DC-6, Trans Mediterranean Airways. OY-BAV Douglas DC-6, Sterling Airways. OY-KRA/ SE-DAF Caravelles, SAS. SE-ERB/E/I/L Douglas DC-7s, Transair Sweden.

✧ **Tue 12 Jul**: 5X-AAO de Havilland Comet 4, East African Airways. 7T-VAK/L Caravelles, Air Algerie. 9700 Bristol 170, Royal Canadian Air Force. CF-CPG Douglas DC-8, Canadian Pacific Air Lines. CF-FUN Boeing 727, Wardair. CF-NAI Douglas DC-7, Pacific Western Airlines. EC-ATV Caravelle, Iberia. G-ALAL Lockheed Constellation, ACE Freighters. G-ARSD Aviation Traders Carvair, British United Air Ferries. HA-MOC Ilyushin IL-18, Malev. HB-AAL Handley Page Herald, Globe Air. HB-ICU Caravelle, Swissair. HB-ILU Douglas DC-4, Balair. I-DIMU Douglas DC-6B, SAM. LN-KLP Caravelle, SAS. N375WA Boeing 707, World Airways. N802SW Douglas DC-8, Seaboard World Airways. OY-BAS Douglas DC-6, Sterling Airways. SE-CNF/G/H Douglas DC-7s, Osterman Air Charter. SE-ERB Douglas DC-7, Transair Sweden. WM739 Percival Sea Prince, Royal Navy.

✧ **Wed 13 Jul**: 972/662/KN269 Dakotas, Royal Canadian Air Force. 9700 Bristol 170, Royal Canadian Air Force. CF-FUN Boeing 727, Wardair. EC-AVZ Caravelle, Iberia. F-BGOB/BGSK/BGSL Douglas DC-6Bs, UTA. F-BHBI/BHMI Lockheed Super Constellations, Air France. F-BHRT/BLKF Caravelles, Air France. F-BILL Douglas DC-4, Air France. G-ALAL Lockheed Constellation, ACE Freighters. G-AMSH Dakota, Irefly. G-AMWW Dakota, Skyways. G-ANMF Bristol 170, British United Air Ferries. G-ARSD Aviation Traders Carvair, British United Air Ferries. HA-MOC Ilyushin IL-18, Malev. HB-IBU/Z Douglas DC-6Bs, Balair. HB-ICW/Y Caravelles, Swissair. HB-ITB Bristol Britannia, Globe Air. I-DIMU Douglas DC-6B, SAM. LN-RTO Dakota, Polaris Air Transport. LN-SUB/D Douglas DC-6s, Braathens SAFE. N17324 Boeing 707, Continental Airlines. N852F Douglas DC-8, Overseas National Airways. N9742Z Lockheed Super Constellation, American Flyers Airline. OE-LAL Vickers Viscount, Austrian Airlines. OY-ANA Douglas DC-7, Internord. OY-EAR Douglas DC-6, Sterling Airways. OY-KRG Caravelle, SAS. SE-CCB Douglas DC-7C, SAS. SE-CNE/F Douglas DC-7s, Osterman Air Charter.

✧ **Thur 14 Jul**: 5A-DAA Caravelle, Kingdom of Libya Airlines. 9700 Bristol 170, Royal Canadian Air Force. EC-ATV Caravelle, Iberia. F-BGOB Douglas DC-6, UTA. G-AOFW Aviation Traders Carvair, British United Air Ferries. HB-IBU Douglas DC-6B, Balair. HB-ICT/X Caravelles, Swissair. HB-ITB Bristol Britannia, Globe Air. I-DIMB Douglas DC-6B, SAM. LN-SUL/W Fokker F-27s, Braathens SAFE. LX-LGZ Lockheed Starliner, Luxair. N8008D Douglas DC-8, Trans International Airlines. OE-LAL Vickers Viscount, Austrian Airlines. OH-KDB Douglas DC-6, Kar-Air. OH-LRF Convair 440, Finnair. OH-LSC Caravelle, Finnair. OY-BAV Douglas DC-6, Sterling Airways. PH-DSO Douglas DC-7C, Martins Air Charter. SE-BDO Douglas DC-6, Transair Sweden. SE-CCB Douglas DC-7C, SAS. SE-CNE/F/H Douglas DC-7s, Osterman Air Charter. SE-DAB Caravelle, SAS. SE-ERI Douglas DC-7, Transair Sweden. WL679 Vickers Varsity, RAF.

✧ **Fri 15 Jul**: EC-ATX/AYE Caravelles, Iberia. EC-BCH Douglas DC-7, Trans-Europa. F-BKBI Bristol 170 Superfreighter, Cie Air Transport. G-ARSD Aviation Traders Carvair, British United Air Ferries. HA-MOA Ilyushin IL-18, Malev. HB-AAK/L Handley Page Heralds, Globe Air. HB-ICA Convair 990A, Swissair. HB-ICT Caravelle, Swissair. I-DIME Douglas DC-6B, SAM. LN-KLR Caravelle, SAS. LN-SUM Douglas DC-6, Braathens SAFE. LX-LGB Fokker F-27, Luxair. N375WA Boeing 707, World Airways. OK-MBB Bristol Britannia, CSA. OY-BAV Douglas DC-6, Sterling Airways. PH-DSC Douglas DC-7C, Martins Air Charter. PH-MAG Dakota, Martins Air Charter. SE-CNE/F/G Douglas DC-7s, Osterman Air Charter. SE-DAD Caravelle, SAS. SE-ERI Douglas DC-7, Transair Sweden. WV735 Percival Pembroke, RAF. XK716 de Havilland Comet C2, RAF. XP823 de Havilland Canada Beaver, Army Air Corps.

✧ **Sat 16 Jul**: 15929 Canadair CC-106 Yukon, Royal Canadian Air Force. 662 Dakota, Royal Canadian Air Force. 5A-DAA Caravelle, Kingdom of Libya Airlines. EC-ATQ Douglas DC-7C, Spantax. EC-AVY Caravelle, Iberia. EC-BCH Douglas DC-7, Trans-Europa. G-ALAK Lockheed Constellation, ACE Freighters. G-AOUV Bristol 170 Superfreighter, British United Air Ferries. G-APEJ Vickers Vanguard, BEA. G-ARSD Aviation Traders Carvair, British United Air Ferries. HB-AAL Handley Page Herald, Globe Air. HB-AAV Fokker F-27, Balair. HB-IBU Douglas DC-6B, Balair. HB-ICU Caravelle, Swissair. I-DIMB/E/I/P/U Douglas DC-6Bs, SAM. LN-KLH/SE-DAF Caravelles, SAS. LX-LGA Fokker F-27, Luxair. N86682 Lockheed Super Constellation, American Flyers Airline. OH-KDB Douglas DC-6, Kar-Air. XP805 de Havilland Canada Beaver, Army Air Corps. YR-IME Ilyushin IL-18, Tarom. YU-AFB Douglas DC-6, Government of Yugoslavia. YU-AFD/E Douglas DC-6s, Adria Airways.

✧ **Sun 17 Jul**: 7T-VAK Caravelle, Air Algerie. CCCP-42459 Tupolev TU-104, Aeroflot. CF-CPG Douglas DC-8, Canadian Pacific Air Lines. EC-ARL/ATV/ AVZ/AYD Caravelles, Iberia. EI-ANO Boeing 707, Aer Lingus. G-ALAK

Lockheed Constellation, ACE Freighters. G-APEC Vickers Vanguard, BEA. G-ARSD Aviation Traders Carvair, British United Air Ferries. HB-IBU Douglas DC-6B, Balair. HB-ICU/W/Z Caravelles, Swissair. I-DIMB/D/E/I Douglas DC-6Bs, SAM. LN-KLH Caravelle, SAS. LX-LGA/B Fokker F-27s, Luxair. LZ-BEN Ilyushin IL-18, TABSO. OY-EAR Douglas DC-6, Sterling Airways. PH-DSL Douglas DC-7C, Martins Air Charter. SE-DAD Caravelle, SAS. TS-MAC/TAR Caravelles, Tunis Air. YU-AFC/E Douglas DC-6s, Adria Airways.

✧ **Mon 18 Jul**: CF-CPG Douglas DC-8, Canadian Pacific Air Lines. EC-ATX/ AVZ/BBR Caravelles, Iberia. EI-ANV Boeing 707, Aer Lingus. G-ASPM Douglas DC-4, Invicta Airways. HB-IBU Douglas DC-6B, Balair. HB-ICX/Y Caravelles, Swissair. I-DIMB Douglas DC-6B, SAM. LN-KLH/SE-DAH Caravelles. SAS. N372WA Boeing 707, World Airways. SE-ERI Douglas DC-7, Transair Sweden. XG496 de Havilland Devon, RAF. XM296 de Havilland Heron, Royal Navy. YU-AHA Caravelle, JAT.

✧ **Tue 19 Jul**: 10319 Canadair CC-106 Yukon, Royal Canadian Air Force. CF-FUN Boeing 727, Wardair. CF-PWM Douglas DC-7, Pacific Western Airlines. EC-ATX Caravelle, Iberia. F-BFUO Bristol 170, Cie Air Transport. G-ANBF Bristol Britannia, Britannia Airways. G-AOUV Bristol 170 Superfreighter, British United Air Ferries. G-ARMX HS-748, Skyways Coach-Air. G-ARRB Boeing 707, BOAC. HA-MOC Ilyushin IL-18, Malev. HB-ICA Convair 990A, Swissair. HB-ILU Douglas DC-4, Balair. JY-ACT Caravelle, Royal Jordanian Airlines. N3325T Douglas DC-8, Trans International Airlines. N376WA Boeing 707, World Airways. OY-BAS/EAR Douglas DC-6s, Sterling Airways. OY-KRG Caravelle, SAS. SE-CNE Douglas DC-7, Osterman Air Charter. SE-ERA Douglas DC-7, Transair Sweden. WL679 Vickers Varsity, RAF. WV749 Percival Pembroke, RAF. XG502 Bristol Sycamore helicopter, RAF.

✧ **Wed 20 Jul**: 662/972/KN269 Dakotas, Royal Canadian Air Force. EC-ATV Caravelle, Iberia. F-BAXR Dakota, Rousseau Aviation. G-ALAK Lockheed Constellation, ACE Freighters. G-ANMF Bristol 170, British United Air Ferries. G-ARSD Aviation Traders Carvair, British United Air Ferries. G-ASPM Douglas DC-4, Invicta Airways. HB-ICY Caravelle, Swissair. HB-ITC Bristol Britannia, Globe Air. I-DIME Douglas DC-6B, SAM. LN-SUI/K Douglas DC-6s, Braathens SAFE. N4905C Douglas DC-8, Capitol International. OH-LSF Caravelle, Finnair. OY-EAR Douglas DC-6, Sterling Airways. OY-KNB/D Douglas DC-7Cs, SAS.

✧ **Thur 21 Jul**: 10302 Lockheed C-130 Hercules, Royal Canadian Air Force. 662/KN269 Dakotas, Royal Canadian Air Force. 9698/9700 Bristol 170s, Royal Canadian Air Force. 5A-DAB Caravelle, Kingdom of Libya Airlines. CCCP-42456 Tupolev TU-104, Aeroflot. EC-ARK/ATV Caravelles, Iberia. EI-AKK Vickers Viscount, Aer Lingus. F-BFUO Bristol 170. G-ALAK/L Lockheed Constellations, ACE Freighters. G-ANBF Bristol Britannia, Britannia Airways.

G-ANBM Bristol Britannia, Laker Airways. G-ANMF Bristol 170, British United Air Ferries. G-APFD/L Boeing 707s, BOAC. G-ARPD HS Trident, BEA. G-ARSD Aviation Traders Carvair, British United Air Ferries. G-ASPM Douglas DC-4, Invicta Airways. HA-MOA/C Ilyushin IL-18s, Malev. HB-AAK Handley Page Herald, Globe Air. HB-IBR Douglas DC-6B, Balair. HB-ICG Convair 990A, Swissair. HB-ICU/Y Caravelles, Swissair. I-DIME Douglas DC-6B, SAM. LN-MOD Douglas DC-7C, SAS. LN-SUK Douglas DC-6, Braathens SAFE. LX-LGZ Lockheed Starliner, Luxair. N373WA Boeing 707, World Airways. N852F Douglas DC-8, Overseas National Airways. OE-LAK Vickers Viscount, Austrian Airlines. OY-EAR Douglas DC-6, Sterling Airways. SE-CNF Douglas DC-7, Osterman Air Charter. SE-DAB Caravelle, SAS. SU-ALC de Havilland Comet 4C, Egyptair (Heathrow diversion).

✧ **Fri 22 Jul**: 10303 Lockheed C-130 Hercules, Royal Canadian Air Force. D-ABAN Douglas DC-7, Sudflug. F-BLHH Bristol 170, Cie Air Transport. HA-MAE Ilyushin IL-14, Malev. LZ-BER Ilyushin IL-18, TABSO. N73675 Douglas DC-7, International Airlines. N851F Douglas DC-8, Overseas National Airways.

✧ **Sat 23 Jul:** 10308 Lockheed C-130 Hercules, Royal Canadian Air Force. 15927 Canadair CC-106 Yukon, Royal Canadian Air Force. EC-BCI Douglas DC-7, Trans Europa. EC-BDM Douglas DC-7C, Spantax. F-BJTR Caravelle, Air France. TC-SEK Fokker F-27, THY Turkish Airlines. XJ324 de Havilland Sea Devon, Royal Navy.

✧ **Sun 24 Jul**: CF-PWM Douglas DC-7, Pacific Western Airlines. LZ-BEP Ilyushin IL-18, TABSO. N3325T Douglas DC-8, Trans International Airlines. OY-DPR de Havilland Heron, Falcks Flyvetjenste.

✧ **Mon 25 Jul**: 5-106 Lockheed C-130 Hercules, Imperial Iranian Air Force. EI-APC Bristol 170, Aer Turas. N375WA Boeing 707, World Airways. N8008D Douglas DC-8, Trans International Airlines.

✧ **Tue 26 Jul**: 10312 Lockheed C-130 Hercules, Royal Canadian Air Force. 15923 Canadair CC-106 Yukon, Royal Canadian Air Force. N17321 Boeing 707, Continental Airlines. N90802 Douglas DC-7C, Saturn Airways.

✧ **Wed 27 Jul**: G-APFL Boeing 707, BOAC. G-ASPM Douglas DC-4, Invicta Airways. I-DIMD Douglas DC-6B, SAM. LN-SUI Douglas DC-6, Braathens SAFE. WM756 Percival Sea Prince, Royal Navy.

✧ **Thur 28 Jul**: TX230 Avro Anson, RAF.

✧ **Fri 29 Jul**: 10309 Canadair CC-106 Yukon, Royal Canadian Air Force. CF-NAI/PWM Douglas DC-7s, Pacific Western Airlines. EI-ANO Boeing 707, Aer Lingus. EI-APC Bristol 170, Aer Turas. G-ALAK Lockheed Constellation, ACE Freighters. G-AOUV Bristol 170 Superfreighter, British United Air Ferries. HB-AAK Handley Page Herald, Globe Air. I-DIMD Douglas DC-6B, SAM. OY-BAT Douglas DC-6, Sterling Airways.

✧ **Sat 30 Jul**: 10309 Lockheed C-130 Hercules, Royal Canadian Air Force. 15929 Canadair CC-106 Yukon, Royal Canadian Air Force. 972 Dakota, Royal Canadian Air Force. CA+103 Lockheed Jetstar, West German Air Force. CF-FUN Boeing 727, Wardair. D-ABAS Douglas DC-7, Sudflug. EC-ATQ Douglas DC-7C, Spantax. F-BAXR Dakota, Rousseau Aviation. G-ALAK Lockheed Constellation, ACE Freighters. G-ANMF Bristol 170, British United Air Ferries. G-APEM Vickers Vanguard, BEA. HA-MOA Ilyushin IL-18, Malev. HB-IBU Douglas DC-6B, Balair. I-DIMB/D/I Douglas DC-6Bs, SAM. N73675 Douglas DC-7, International Airlines. N8008D Douglas DC-8, Trans International Airlines. N852F Douglas DC-8, Overseas National Airways. N90802 Douglas DC-7C, Saturn Airways. OH-KDA Douglas DC-6, Kar-Air. PH-CGD Convair 640, Martins Air Charter. SE-CFA/D Curtis C-46 Commandos, Tor Air. VQ-ZEC Douglas DC-4, Bechuanaland National Airways. YR-IMD Ilyushin IL-18, Tarom. YU-AFF Douglas DC-6, Adria Airways.

✧ **Sun 31 Jul**: 7T-VAI/L Caravelles, Air Algerie. CCCP-42508 Tupolev TU-104, Aeroflot. EC-BBR Caravelle, Iberia. HB-ICH Convair 990A, Swissair. HB-IDA Douglas DC-8, Swissair. LN-KLP Caravelle, SAS. LX-LGB Fokker F-27, Luxair. LZ-BEM Ilyushin IL-18, TABSO. N374WA Boeing 707, World Airways.

APPENDIX 7

TABLE OF PASSENGERS AND FREIGHT HANDLED AND AIRCRAFT MOVEMENTS, FROM THE REOPENING IN 1958 UNTIL 1977

Passengers Handled:

Year	Scheduled	Non-Scheduled	Transit	Total
1958/59	163,977	55,248	134	219,359
1959/60	229,711	140,188	1,931	371,830
1960/61	260,877	222,583	5,647	489,107
1961/62	373,781	490,062	8,949	872,792
1962/63	351,258	687,279	3,544	1,042,081
1963/64	254,369	726,852	3,536	984,757
1964/65	285,161	851,224	4,029	1,140,414
1965/66	376,959	1,031,338	10,181	1,418,478
1966/67	586,734	1,047,306	15,802	1,649,842
1967/68	614,443	1,354,638	8,300	1,977,381
1968/69	603,289	1,507,504	12,021	2,122,814
1969/70	681,655	2,437,622	19,323	3,138,600
1970/71	729,157	3,094,868	26,362	3,850,387
1971/72	923,142	4,046,996	45,887	5,016,025
1972/73	1,167,799	4,223,616	56,694	5,448,109
1973/74	1,455,832	4,221,919	54,637	5,732,388
1974/75	1,460,860	3,653,151	58,656	5,172,667
1975/76	1,364,654	3,977,906	68,005	5,410,565
1976/77	1,491,082	4,404,600	40,071	5,935,753

Aircraft Movements and Cargo Handled:

Year	Air Transport	General Aviation	Other	Total Movements	Cargo (metric tonnes)
1958/59	11,697	497	1,920	14,114	5,313
1959/60	15,937	1,599	8,245	25,781	7,672
1960/61	20,094	3,212	14,328	37,634	8,750
1961/62	25,700	4,141	14,098	43,939	9,215
1962/63	26,242	5,613	12,089	43,944	8,188
1963/64	25,362	8,309	12,603	46,274	11,161
1964/65	27,559	10,769	14,763	53,091	11,663
1965/66	29,422	12,476	18,182	60,080	13,757
1966/67	33,779	14,521	18,347	66,647	16,543
1967/68	37,818	16,801	15,705	70,324	18,896
1968/69	38,453	17,796	19,123	75,372	23,052
1969/70	50,641	20,479	18,017	89,137	25,908
1970/71	54,603	23,487	15,811	93,901	33,557
1971/72	68,330	23,105	13,496	104,931	38,708
1972/73	73,934	20,985	11,999	106,918	44,275
1973/74	74,598	23,085	12,669	110,352	47,579
1974/75	72,540	21,616	11,250	105,406	58,329
1975/76	74,669	18,969	12,639	106,277	77,811
1976/77	81,503	15,592	12,247	109,342	83,304

(Source: BAA)

BIBLIOGRAPHY

During the preparation of this book, reference was made to the following sources, all of which are highly recommended for further study, but some of which are unfortunately out of print:

Books

Allward, M., *London's Airports – Heathrow And Gatwick* (Ian Allan Publishing).

Jones, G., *Gatwick Airport* (Ian Allan Publishing, 2000).

King, J., *Gatwick – The Evolution of an Airport* (Gatwick Airport Ltd and Sussex Industrial Archaeology Society, 1986).

King, J. and Tait, G., *Golden Gatwick* (RAes Gatwick Branch and BAA, 1980).

Merton Jones, A.C., *British Independent Airlines Since 1946* (vols 1–4, first edition) (Merseyside Aviation Society Ltd and LAAS International, 1976).

Simons, G., *Gatwick – From a Flying Club to a Major Hub* (2010).

Simons, G., *The Spirit of Dan-Air* (GMS Enterprises, 1993).

Thaxter, D., *The History Of British Caledonian Airways 1928–1988* (2011).

Other Sources

Aviation Safety Network website (for accident reports).

Flight Global Archive website (period articles from *Flight International* magazine).

Gatwick Aviation Society website (for airport history details and historical aircraft movements).

Grand National website (for details of Grand National races run at Gatwick Racecourse).

Hawkeye magazine (various issues). Gatwick Aviation Society.

Various BAA press releases and publications.

Visit our website and discover thousands of other History Press books.

www.thehistorypress.co.uk